JAVANESE
Dictionary
&
Phrasebook

JAVANESE
Dictionary & Phrasebook

Compiled by
Siti Nur'Aini

Hippocrene Books, Inc.
New York

For information, address:
HIPPOCRENE BOOKS, INC.
171 Madison Ave.
New York, NY 10016
www.hippocrenebooks.com

Library of Congress Cataloging-in-Publication Data

Nur'aini, Siti (Lexicographer), compiler.
Javanese-English/English-Javanese dictionary &
phrasebook / compiled by Siti Nur'aini.
pages cm
ISBN 978-0-7818-1328-0 (pbk.)
ISBN 0-7818-1328-X (pbk.)
1. Javanese language--Dictionaries--English. 2. English language--Dictionaries--Javanese. 3. Javanese language--Conversation and phrase books--English. I. Title. II. Title: Javanese-English/English-Javanese dictionary and phrasebook.
PL5166N87 2015
499'.222321--dc23

2014002401

Printed in the United States of America.

ABBREVIATIONS

adj.	adjective
adv.	adverb
conj.	conjunction
interj.	interjection
n.	noun
pron.	pronoun
v.	verb

INTRODUCTION TO THE JAVANESE LANGUAGE

Javanese is the language of the Javanese people, and is predominantly spoken in the Central and Eastern parts of the Indonesian island of Java. It is part of the Austronesian language culture and shares many common features with nearby languages such as Sundanese, Malay, Madurese, Dayak, and Bugisian. Javanese also has strong influences from the languages of West Madagascar, Taiwan, and New Zealand. There are an estimated 82 million Javanese speakers and the language is ranked as the eleventh most-spoken worldwide.

The modern-day Javanese language descends from a long line of related Javanese languages, stretching back to *Purba*, or Old Javanese, which has preserved writings stretching all the way back to the ninth century. Strongly influenced by Hinduism and Buddhism, the introduction and gradual cultural dominance of Islam to the region lead to significant developments in the language, including the adoption of Arabic vocabularies and a diminished influence from Sanskrit on the written language.

Contact with the Dutch further developed the language to its current form, where native Javanese terms are freely mixed with Arab, Dutch, and English loanwords. As Indonesia becomes more and more integral to the world economy,

Javanese is increasingly taking on prominence on the global linguistic stage and continues to adapt with new vocabulary words and colloquialisms borrowed from other regional and international languages.

Politeness in Javanese

Javanese as a spoken language maintains a careful acknowledgment of levels of politeness, known as *unggah-ungguh* or *tata krama*. This tradition can be traced to the highly influential historical kingdom Sultan Agung, which established levels of respect to be used when addressing individuals of higher or lower rank.

There are three main levels of politeness in Javanese: *ngoko* (familiar), *madya* (general), and *krama* (honorific). In each level, there is a form of "honoring" the listener, which is called *ngajengaken*, as well as a way of addressing those of lower position, known as *ngasoraken*. It is common for Javanese speakers to change the level of politeness used in their speech to account for relative social statuses of both the speaker and the listener, with status most typically determined by age, occupation, and rank. For example, a young child typically converses with friends using *ngoko*, but will address his parents with *krama*.

This system of politeness is commonly used in Surakarta, Yogyakarta, and Madiun, but is less popular in other areas of Java. Two other levels of speech, *bagongan* and *kedhaton*, are primarily only used within the palace when addressing members of the royal family.

Below are a few examples of politeness variations on the English phrase “Excuse me, I’d like to ask you, where is Budi’s house?”

Ngoko lugu:
“Eh, aku arep takon, omahé Budi kuwi, nèng ndi? (A conversation between two persons who are peers or friends.)

Ngoko alus:
“Aku nyuwun pirsa, dalemé mas Budi kuwi, nèng endi?” (Stranger asking directions of another stranger of the same age.)

Self-aggrandizing ngoko:
“Aku kersa ndangu, omahé mas Budi kuwi, nèng ndi?” (This is considered to be impolite in Javanese society. One cannot use *krama inggil* lexicon to talk about himself because it is rude, insensitive, and it reflects one’s sense of self-importance.)

Madya alus:
“Nuwun sèwu, kula ajeng tanglet, dalemé mas Budi niku, teng pundi?” (Stranger asking another stranger who is older or has higher social status.)

Krama alus:
“Nuwun sewu, kula badhe nyuwun pirsa, dalemipun mas Budi punika, wonten pundi?” (Stranger asking another stranger who is older. The person who asks is from a middle or upper level in the society and likely well-educated.)

Since much of the differences in level of speech are based on vocabulary choice, not grammatical structure, speakers will have to learn on their own the vocabularies of the different levels and how to employ them. When in doubt, it is recommended that newcomers to the language use the most polite speech. The phrases given in this book all use the *krama* level of politeness.

Javanese Dialects

The mountainous, disconnected nature of the Indonesian archipelago has ensured a great amount of linguistic variation across the region, even within a single language like Javanese. This dictionary uses the combination of Surakartan and Yogyakartan dialects, as the two cities in Central Java province are the standard reference for formal use of the Javanese language. Formal Javanese is used in text books, newspapers, or other publications for public reading. Examples of the dialect are as follow:

Adik kula ndawahaken piring.
(My sister dropped the plate.)
This is the formal use of language. The basic word for *ndawahaken* is "*dawah*" which means "to fall, to drop." This is a standard word used by people in Surakarta and Yogyakarta regions.

Adik kula nyeblokaken piring.
(My sister dropped the plate.)
This is a common dialectal variant of

the above sentence. The root word for *nyeblokaken* is "*ceblok*," which is commonly used in the regions of Pati, Kudus, Juwana, and some other cities in the northern part of Central Java.

Javanese Grammar and Tenses

Unlike many European languages, Javanese does not conjugate or otherwise alter the verb or subject to express a change in tense, but instead relies on time markers. The verb forms, subject of a sentence, and sentence structure remain the same regardless of whether the speaker is communicating past, present, or simple tenses—the time reference alone is sufficient to communicate when the event or action occurred.

Examples:

Present tense
Ibu dhahar sarapan.
(Mother is having breakfast.)
The event is happening at the moment of speaking.

Past tense
Ibu ***sampun*** *dhahar sarapan.*
(Mother had breakfast.)
"*Sampun*" here is a time reference that indicates the event when mother ate the breakfast happened in the past.

Indefinite future tense

Adhi ***badhé*** *sowan dateng griyanipun pak lurah.*

(Adhi will visit the village head's house.)

"*Badhé*" gives time reference of activities that will be done in the future, but since it does not have a time marker, the time of the visit is unknown. He will visit, but he hasn't decided when.

Definite future tense

Sinar ***badhé*** *tindak Jakarta* ***mangkih dalu tabuh 8.***

(Sinar is going to Jakarta tonight at 8.)

"*Badhé*" gives time reference of activities that will be done in the future. The added date and time indicates a definite plan.

THE JAVANESE ALPHABET

Javanese people credit the creation of their alphabet to a famous hero named Ajisaka, who established the kingdom of Medang Kamulan. While campaigning against his enemies, Ajisaka left his faithful retainer Dora on the island of Majethi with a powerful weapon, telling him not to give the weapon to anybody except those he personally instructed him to entrust it to. After finishing his war and becoming king, Ajisaka sent another retainer, Sembada, to retrieve the weapon. Since Dora had not been personally informed by Ajisaka to give Sembada the weapon, and since Sembada could not return without it, the two men fought and killed each other. Since each had just been fulfilling their duties but died because of a problem of communication, Ajisaka decided to honor their legacies by creating the Javanese alphabet, so that further miscommunications would not lead to such needless loss in the future.

Today, most Javanese remember the myth of Dora and Sembada, with a short poem that also cleverly reflects the alphabetical order of the Javanese alphabet:

Ha Na Ca Ra Ka there were two messengers
Da Ta Sa Wa La they were fighting
Pa Dha Ja Ya Nya both were powerful
Ma Ga Ba Tha Nga both died

Today, Javanese uses Latin script, not the flowing cursive letters credited to Ajisaka. The following chart gives a guide to the sound of each letter, along with its closest English approximation:

Javanese Consonants

Consonants	English Approximation
h	horse
n	now
c	chair
r	river
ḳ	kitten
d	duck
t	table
s	sing
w	week
l	long
p	pan
dh	do
j	judge
y	you
ny	new
m	mother
g	guy
b	book
th	attack
ng	singing

Javanese Vowels

Vowels	English Approximation
a	car
ạ	law
i	pit
u	ruse
è	turn
é	egg
e	prey
o	role
ọ	dog

JAVANESE-ENGLISH DICTIONARY

A

abad century
abrit red
abuh swelling
adegan scene
adil even
administrasi administration
agami religion
ageman shirt; **ageman siram** bathing suit
agen agent
ageng big, large
agensi agency (*n.*)
Agustus August
AIDS AIDS
air mancur fountain
ajrih afraid
akademi academy
akomodasi accommodation
aksèn accent
akte klairan birth certificate
aktivis activist
aktor actor
aktual actual
akun account
akuntan accountant
akurat accurate
alamat address (*n.*)
alarm alarm; **alarm kebakaran** fire alarm
alergi allergy
alesanipun reason
ali-ali ring
alit little, small
alkohol alcohol
almon almond
alon slow
altar altar (*n.*)
alus mild; smooth, soft
amargi because of
ambal warsa birthday, anniversary
ambegan breathe (*v.*)
ambet odor
ambu smell
ambulan ambulance
Amérika Serikat United States
amplop envelope
amurub on
andha stairs
andhap low
andhuk towel; **anduk kagem siram** bath towel
anemia anemic
anget warm
anggota member
anggur grape; wine
angin lésus storm
angkatan laut navy
angkutan umum public transportation
angsal get; **angsal mancing** fishing permitted
antibeku antifreeze
antiseptik antiseptic

antibiotik antibiotics
antik antique
antri queue
apartemèn apartment
apel apple
apotik drugstore
aprikot apricot
April April
apus krama trick (*n.*)
are (0,4 hektar) acre (0.4 hectares)
arsitèktur architecture
arta money; **arta tunai** cash (*n.*)
asem sour
asep smoke
asli original; pure
asma asthma; name, **asma kaluarga** surname
aspirin aspirin
asrep cold
asring always; often (*adv.*)
asta hand
asuransi insurance; **asuransi kesehatan** health insurance
ATM ATM
atos hard
atusan hundred
aula hall
awak body
awakipun piyambak our
awis expensive
awon bad
awrat heavy

B

babagan chapter
babi pig
bagasi luggage
bahan bakar fuel
bal ball; **bal basket** basketball
bal-balan soccer, football
balung bone
ban tire; **ban bocor** flat tire
bandara airport
bangsa nation
banjir flood
bank bank
bantal pillow
banthèng bull
bantuan arah directory assistance
bapak father
bar bar
barang item, thing
barang-barang goods
basa language; **basa Inggris** English language; **basa manca** foreign languages
bata brick
batal cancel
baterai battery

bathi profit
baut screw
bawang pethak onion
bayi baby
béa cukai customs
béaya (*n.*) charge, cost, fee; **bèaya mlebet** cover charge
bèbas free; **bèbas pajek** duty-free
bebaya danger, hazzard; disaster
bebelen constipated
bedhil gun
beja fortune
bekas second
beksa dance
beku frozen
bèl bell
bendungan reservoir
bengkel repair shop
bènsin gasoline, petrol
bènten different
bentèr hot; heat
berburu hunt
berkah bless
berri berry
beton concrete
biarawati nun
biasa ordinary, usual (*adj.*)
biji score
bingkisan parcel
bioskop cinema, movie theater
bir beer
birokrasi bureaucracy
biru blue
bis bus
bisnis business
bistik steak
blanja expense
bledhèk thunder
blèk jar
bobot weigh
bolongan hole
bolpèn pen
bom bomb
bonus bonus
bosok rotten
botol bottle
bréngos moustache
brontak rebel
budhal departure
budhaya culture
budheg deaf
bujang single (*n.*)
buku book; **buku panduan** guidebook
bulan madu honeymoon
bumi earth
bundel knot
bunder circle

C

cacat disability; disabled
cacing worm
cahya light
caket close (*adv.*)

campuran mix
candhi temple
cangkir cup
cangkriman puzzle
caos sauce
caraka messenger
cathetan note
CD CD
cek check (*n.*)
cekap enough
celak near (*prep.*), nearby (*adj.*); **celak kaliyan** next to
cemeng black
cendhèk short
cendhéla window
cepet express, quick, rapid; speed
check in check in
check out check out
cidra lie
ciut narrow
clana pants; **clana jins** jeans
coklat chocolate
cokot bite
cokotan srangga insect bite
colong steal
cuaca weather

D

dados become (*v.*)
dagangan trade
daging meat; **daging cèlèng** pork; **daging sapi** beef
daleman underwear
dalu night; **dalu punika** tonight
dandan dress (*v.*)
daptar list
darurat emergency
dasar base
dasi tie
dawah down
dedonga pray
dékade decade
démokrasi democracy
denda penalty, sanction
dengkul knee
déodoran deodorant
deposito deposit
depot depot
dèrètan suite
Désember December
dhahar eat; **dhahar dalu** dinner; **dhahar siyang** lunch
dhaharan dish, food, meal; **dhaharan cepet saji** fast food; **dhaharan dalu** dine; **dhaharan laut** seafood; **dhaharan panutup** dessert
dhawah fall
dhayoh visitor
dhèk deck
dhèwèké they

diagnosa diagnosis
diare diarrhea
digarang roasted
dingklik chair
dinten day; **dinten makaryo** weekday; **dinten punika** today; **Dinten Warsa Énggal** New Year's Day
dipan bed
diplomat diplomat
dipun lek swallow (*v.*)
dipun lengkapi furnished
dipun olah malih recycle
dipun parengaken allowed
dipun ungsiaken evacuate
direktori directory
disel diesel
diskon discount
distrik district
diwasa adult
diyan lamp
dluwang paper
dobel double
dok dock
dokter doctor, physician; **dokter bedhah** surgeon; **dokter gigi** dentist
dokumèn document
dolanan game; play (*v.*)
dolar dollar
dom needle
domestik domestic
dompèt purse, wallet
donya world
dosin dozen
DPR legislature
drama drama
duka angry
dumugi come; until (*conj.*)
duta besar ambassador
DVD DVD
dwija teacher, tutor

E

éca delicious
édan mad (*adj.*)
eja spell
ekonomi economy
ekstra extra
éling remember
email e-mail
emas gold
èncèr liquid
endut mud
enem six
enembelas sixteen
ener direction; directions
ènggal- ènggal hurry; eventually
énggal new (*adj.*); soon (*adv.*)
enjing morning

entri entry
epilepsi epileptic
Éropa Europe
es ice
eskalator escalator
èstri female, lady
etnis ethnic
ewet complicated, difficult
èyang kakung grandfather
èyang putri grandmother

F

faksimili fax (*n.*)
farmasi pharmacy
fasilitas amenities
festival festival
film film, movie
formulir béa cukai customs declaration
foto photograph
frasa phrase

G

gagang pancing fishing rod
gajian payment
galak wild
gambar picture
gampil dibeta portable (*adj.*)
gandhum wheat
gang aisle; **gang alit** alley
gangsal five; **gangsal welas** fifteen
ganti change (*n.*)
gantos exchange
garing dry (*adj.*)
garpu fork
garwa èstri wife
garwa kakung husband
gatel itch
gaun dress (*n.*)
gegambar wontentembok mural
gegar otak concussion
gegayutan relationship
gegeman fist
geger back
gejala symptom
gelas glass
genah confirm
gendéra flag
gendhis sugar
geni fire
gerah illness; sick; **gerah talingan** earache; **gerah waja** toothache
gesang alive (*adj.*); life (*n.*); live (*v.*)
ginjel kidney
gir gear
giri mount

glepung flour
golongan darah blood type
graji saw
gram gram
grana nose
gréja church; **gréja alit** chapel
griya home, house; **griya sakit** hospital
gujeng laugh
gunggung amount (*n.*)
gunting scissors
gunung alit hill
gurita octopus
guwo cave
gym gym

H

hadhiah prize
haid menstruation
hak asasi manungsa human rights
hakim judge
halo hello
hama pest
hei hey (*interj.*)
heteroseksual heterosexual
hiu shark
HIV HIV
homoseksual homosexual
hormat respect
hotel hotel

I

ibu mother; **ibu marasepuh** mother-in-law
ical lost
identifikasi identification
idiom idiom
iga rib
ijem green
ijin permission, license, permit; **ijin mancing** fishing license
iklan advertisement
imigran immigrant
imigrasi immigration
impor import
inciman threat
individual individual
infeksi infection
infrastruktur infrastructure
ing antawisipun among
ing nginggil above
inggih OK
inggih yes; **inggih punika** be (*v.*, am, is, are, was, were, been)
inggil tall; top
ingkang kagungan owner
ingkang nyèwa tenant
ingon-ingon pet
injil bible

insinyur engineer
instan instant
insulin insulin
internasional international
internet Internet; **internet nirkabel** wireless Internet
interpretasi interpretation
istirahat rest

J

jadual schedule
jadwal itinerary
jagung corn
jahitan stitch
jajanan cake; snack (*n.*)
jaket jacket
jalan lingkar detour
jalan tol highway
jalur lane, path
jam clock; o'clock; **jam malam** curfew
jamban lavatory
jampi medicine, cure, remedy (*n.*); herb
jamur mushroom
jangga neck
jangkah step
janji appointment
jantung heart
Januari January
jarang rare
jarum suntik syringe
jawab reply
jawah rain
jempol thumb
jené yellow
jero deep
jeruk lemon lemon
jeruk limau lime
jiplakan copy
jladrènan dough
jogan floor
jujur honest
Juli July
jumeneng stand
Jumuah Friday
jungkat comb
Juni June
jurang cliff
jurnalis journalist
juru basa interpreter
juru ladèn servant
juru ladhèn operator
jus juice

K

kaadilan justice
kabel cable, cord, wire; **kabel jumper** jumper cables; **kabel TV** cable TV
kaca mirror; page; **kaca tingal** eyeglasses
kacang nuts; **kacang**

dawa chickpeas; **kacang polong** bean; **kacang polong** pea; **kacang tanah** peanuts
kacatingal eyeglasses
kacolong stolen
kadadosan event
kadal lizard
kados pundi why (*adv.*)
kadospundi how
kadurjanan crime
kafé cafe
kagèt surprise
kagiyatan activity
kagungan kualitas qualify
kagungan property
kagunganipun piyambak private property
kain cloth, fabric
kainggilan altitude
kajeng wood; **kajeng bakar** firewood
kakuwatan energy
kala dalu overnight (*adv.*)
kala wingi yesterday
kalah lose
kalamangga spider
kalènder calendar
kalih dasa twenty
kalih welas twelve
kaliyan and
kalung necklace
kaluwihan dosis overdose
kamar room, bedroom; **kamar gantos** changing room; **kamar pas** fitting room
kamèra camera
kamus dictionary
kanan right (*direction*)
kanca associate (*n.*); **kanca jaler raket** boyfriend
kandhang cage
kang mas brother
kanthong kagem saré sleeping bag
kantor office; **kantor polisi** police station; **kantor pos** post office
kapal fèri ferry
kaping kalih twice (*adv.*)
kapisah separate (*adj.*)
kapustakan library
kaputusan decision
karantina quarantine
karcis tindhak-kondur round-trip ticket
karèt rubber
karpèt carpet, rug
kasar rough; rude
kaslametan safety
kasur mattress
kasut sock
kata sandi password

katedral cathedral
katentreman security
kathah many, much (*adv.*)
katingal seem (*v.*)
katiwasan accident
katresnan romance
katun cotton
katutup closed
kawates restricted (*adj.*)
kawicaksanaan wisdom
kayu manis cinnamon
kebak full
kebon garden (*n.*); **kebon woh-wohan** orchard
kebrangas sunburn
kebun binatang zoo
kedahipun ought
kedelé soy
kedutaan embassy
kehidupan malam nightlife
kejawi except
kèju cheese
kekerasan violence
kekiatan power
kelas class; **kelas setunggal** first-class
keleresan truth
kelistrikan electric
kémah camp
kembang api fireworks
Kemis Thursday
kemlaratan poverty
kempalan group
kemul blanket
kencing manis diabetic
kendharaan vehicle
kendhi jug
kendo loose
kenging infeksi infected
kenthang potato
kenya girl
kepanggih find
keplok clap
keponakan èstri niece
keponakan jaler nephew
keracunan dhaharan food poisoning
keraméan crowd
kerang mussels, shellfish
keranjang blanja shopping basket
kèrem drown
kerèta cart
kereta bawah tanah subway
kerisakan damage
kernèt conductor
kertas alumunium aluminum foil
kertu card; **kertu krédit** credit card; **kertu pos** postcard; **kertu tèlpon** phone card
kerudung veil (*n.*)
kesabaran patience

kesadé sold; **kesadé telas** sold out
kesehatan health
kètèl kettle
ketiga summer
ketingal appear
khusus special
kidul south
kilat flash
kilen west
kilogram kilogram
kilometer kilometer
kimia chemical
kirang less (*adv.*, little)
kita we (*pron.*)
kitha city
klambu mosquito net
klasik classic
klelep sink
klinik clinic
klub club
kode negari country code
kode panggilan dialing code
kode pos postal code
koin coin
koki chef
kokoa cocoa
kol lettuce
kolam renang pool
komisi commission
kompa pump
kompensasi compensation
kompor stove
kompromi compromise
komputer computer
kondom condom
konferènsi conference
konsèr concert
konstitusi constitution
konsulat consulate
konsultasi consult
kontrak contract
kontrasèpsi contraception
kontrasèptip contraceptive
koper baggage, trunk, suitcase
kopi coffee
korèng scar
korup corrupt
kosher kosher
kosmètik cosmetics
kotak box (*n.*); **kotak pos** postbox; **kotak tèlpon** phone booth
kothong empty
krama married; marry
kraman rebellion
kramat sacred
krambil coconut
kran faucet
kranjang basket
krasan comfortable
krédit credit
kreteg bridge
krim cream; **krim cukur** shaving cream
kringet sweat

kruk crutches
KTP ID card
kualitas quality
kuantitas quantity (*n.*)
kucing cat
kula I (*pron.*)
kulawarga family
kulit leather; skin
kulkas refrigerator
kumbah wash
kumbahan laundry
kunci key
kunjara jail, prison
kursi rodha wheelchair
kutha town
kwitansi receipt

L

labèl tag
ladèn serve
lalu lintas traffic
lampu kilat fotografi flash photography
lancar fluent
landhep sharp
langganan client, customer
langit sky
langkung more (*adv.*), excess; **langkung remen** prefer
lapangan field
larahan dirt, litter, trash
laré child, kid; **laré bayi** infant; **laré èstri** daughter; **laré jaler** boy, son
lathi lip
lawa bat
lawang door
layanan kamar room service
layar sail; screen
lebu ash
lelara disease
lelucon comedy
lèm glue
lemak fat
lemari kaca cabinet
lembaga institution
lemut mosquito
lengen arm
lenggah sit
lensa lens
lepat false, incorrect, wrong; guilty
lèpèn river
leptop laptop
lèr north; **lèr kilèn** northwest; **lèr wétan** northeast
lèrèkan zipper
leres true, correct (*adj.*)
liburan holiday
lift elevator
liga league
lindhu earthquake
lingkungan neighborhood

lisan oral
listrik electricity
liter liter
lobi lobby
logam metal
logat accent
lokal local
lowongan vacancy
lulur spine
lumantar through
lurus straight
luwé hungry

M

mabuk motion sickness; **mabuk laut** seasick
mabur fly
macem kind
madharan stomach
madosi seek
madu honey
majikan employer
makam cemetery
maksimal maximum
Malem Warsa énggal New Year's Eve
malih again
maling thief
mamah chew
mambu banger rot (*v.*)
manah soul
manca foreign
mancing fishing
mandheg halt, stop
mandhégani chief (*adj.*)
mangertos understand, know
mangg èn stay
mangké later
mangkok basin
mangsa climate
mangsi ink
manis sweet
mantel coat
manual manual (*n.*)
manuk dara pigeon
manungsa human
maos read
marengaken allow
margi road, street; **margi ageng** avenue; **margi landai** ramp; **margi mlebet** access; **margi mlebet** entrance
maringi give; **maringi pirsa** show; **maringi salju** snow (*v.*); **maringi wates** limit (*v.*)
maruta wind
masak cook
masalah trouble
maskapai airline
masuk akal reasonable
mata uang currency; **mata uang manca** foreign currency
matematika math
matur nuwun thank you

mbalèaken arta refund
mbandingaken compare
mbantah deny; dispute (*v.*)
mbanyu fluid; melt (*v.*)
mbayar paid; pay; **mbayar malih** repay; **mbayar tunai** cash (*v.*)
mbebayani harm
mbenjang punapa when
mbénjing tomorrow
mbeta bring
mbetahaken require, need (*v.*)
mbikak open; **mbikak kunci** unlock
mbilas flush
mbiyantu assist, help
mboten no; **mboten cekap** insufficient; **mboten kalebet** exclude; **mboten kulina** unusual; **mboten lepat** innocent; **mboten nate** never; **mboten ngeses** non-smoking; **mboten pasti** relative; **mboten remen** unhappy; **mboten sadar** unconscious; **mboten sarujuk** disagree; **mboten sekéca** uncomfortable; **mboten sopan** impolite; **mboten tepang** unfamiliar; **mboten wonten** nothing; **mboten wonten pundi-pundi** nowhere (*adv.*)
mbungkus pack, wrap (*v.*)
medal exit; out (*adv.*); **medal rahipun** bleed
medèni scary (*adj.*)
méja table, desk; **meja ngajeng** front desk
mejahi kill
mekanik mechanic
melon melon
menang win
menawi if; might; possibly, probably
mendem drunk
mèndha goat; sheep
mendhem bury
mendo lamb
mèngeti warn
menit minute
mentah raw
méntal mental
mentèga butter
menu menu
mèsem smile
mesin engine, machine; **mesin cuci** washing machine
mesjid mosque

meter meter
mie noodles
migren migraine
mijet massage
mikir thought
mikrowave microwave
mil mile
milih select (*v.*); **milih swanten** vote
militer military
mimis bullet
mindhahaken move (*v.*)
minggah climb; hike; up (*adv.*)
minggu week
minimal minimum
minor minor (*adj.*)
mint mint
minuman keras liquor
mirah inexpensive, cheap
mireng hear
mirengaken listen
mirsani look; **mirsani gawanan** baggage check
misahaken separate (*v.*)
misteri mystery
miwiti start
mlajeng run
mlampah walk
mlebet enter
mlepuh blister
mlumpat jump
mobil car
montor automobile; motor; **montor mabur** airplane, plane
motèl motel
motong cut
mriang fever
mrica pepper
mriksa check (*v.*)
mriksa examine
mudha young (*adj.*)
mules nausea
mumet dizzy
mundhut purchase, buy, take
mungsuh enemy
mungsuhan hostile
muntah vomit
murub flame
museum museum
musik music
musim season; **musim gugur** autumn
musiman seasonal (*adj.*)
Muslim Muslim
mustaka head
mutusaken decide

N

nadi pulse
nalika moment
nalika period
nambah add
nampan tray

nampi accept, receive
namung just, only
nanging but (*conj.*)
nangis cry
narik appeal, pull; withdraw
narikaken withdrawal
naté ever
navigasi navigation
nbengok yell
ndaftaraken admit
ndamel make (*v.*); use (*v.*); **ndamel beku** freeze; **ndamel janji** promise (*v.*)
ndandosi fix, repair
ndelikaken conceal
ndèrèk join
ndikté dictate
nedahaken exhibit (*v.*)
negari country
nelasaken spend
nelayan fisherman
némbak shoot (*v.*); shot
nembang sing
nendhang kick
nepangaken piyambak introduce oneself
nepsu dhahar appetite
nerjang trespassing
nerjemahaken interpret
nerjemahaken translate
netral neutral (*adj.*)
ngagem wear (*v.*)
ngajeng front
ngambali repeat
ngambung kiss
ngandhap bottom (*n.*)
ngandhut pregnant
ngangkut transport
ngantuk drowsy
ngapik-apik flourish
ngapunten sorry
ngapura forgive
ngasta carry
ngaturaken pronounce (*v.*)
ngaturi pirsa report
ngayomi protect
ngèkspor export
ngelak thirsty
ngelap lebu dust (*v.*)
ngélingaken remind
ngemat load (*v.*)
ngempalaken collect
ngendhika say, tell, speak
ngéngingi about
ngentosi wait
ngethuk knock
nggadhahi own (*v.*)
ngganggu disturb
ngganti change (*v.*)
nggantos replace
nggaringaken dry (*v.*)
nggorèng fry
ngidentifikasi identify
ngijinaken permit (*v.*)
ngina insult
ngindari avoid
nginfeksi infect
nginspeksi inspect

nginten-inten estimate
ngirim deliver
ngirimaken send; **ngirimaken serat** mail (*v.*)
ngisi fill
ngladèni service
nglajengaken carry-on
nglampahi do
nglanggar illegal
nglangi swim
nglarang prohibit
nglawan against
nglebetaken wonten-kotak box (*v.*)
nglilir awake
ngrajut knit
ngrampok rob (*v.*)
ngraos feel
ngraosaken taste
ngrawat treat
ngrekam record, tape
ngrèmèhaken ignore
ngrisak break (*v.*)
ngrokok smoking
ngukum punish
ngunci lock
ngundang invite
ngundhang summon
ngunjuk drink (*v.*)
ngupakara laré childcare
nguras drain
ngurung lock out
ngutil shoplifting
nikah marriage
nilai tukar exchange rate
nimbali call (*v.*)
ningali see, watch; sightseeing
ninggalaken left
nitih ride
njahit sew
njawi ruangan outdoor
njebak trap (*v.*)
njlèntrèhaken explain
njotos punch
njunjung lift
Nn. Ms. (*title*)
nol zero
nomer number; **nomer kursi** seat number; **nomer penerbangan** flight number; **nomer tèlpon** phone number
Nopember November
normal normal
nota pesadéyan sales receipt
nuduh accuse
nuklir nuclear (*adj.*)
nular contagious
nundha postpone; undo
nuntut prosecute
nutup shut, close (*v.*)
nutupi cover; vein
nuwèni visit
nuwun sewu please
Ny. Mrs. (*title*)
nyababaken gatel irritate

nyadaraken revive (*v.*)
nyadé sell (*v.*)
nyaman convenient
nyambut welcome; **nyambut damel** work
nyaranaken recommend
nyatakaken declare, state
nyekik choke
nyenengi like (*v.*)
nyenengken fun
nyenggol touch
nyepeng catch (*v.*)
nyerat write
nyetir drive
nyéwa rent
nyiksa torture
nyilem dive
nyimpen store, keep, reserve
nyinggahaken save
nyinggung manah offend
nyingkiraken remove
nylametaken rescue
nyobi try
nyolokaken plug
nyukur shave
nyulik kidnap
nyuntak pour
nyunthik inject
nyuwèk rip
nyuwun pangapunten apologize

O

obat drug; **obat bius** anesthetic; **obat penenang** sedative
obéng screwdriver
odol toothpaste
oksigen oxygen
Oktober October
olah raga sport(s)
oli oil
ontran-ontran riot
opera opera
oranye orange
organ organ
organik organic
orkestra orchestra
otomatis automatic
otot muscle
oven oven

P

P3K first-aid kit
pacar èstri girlfriend
padésan suburb, village
padhang pasir desert
padhas rock (*n.*)
padosan search (*n.*)
padudon argue
padusan bathroom
pagelaran play (*n.*); theater
pager fence
pai pie

pait bitter
pajar dawn
pajek toll, tax; **pajek bandara** airport tax; **pajek penjualan** sales tax
pak lik uncle
pakaryan occupation
pakèt package
pakiwan toilet
palarapan forehead
palsu fraud
pamarèntah government
pambedhahan surgery
pamilih selection
pamomong bayi babysitter
panci pan
pancuran shower
pandhita priest
panduan guide (*n.*)
pangapunten pardon (*n.*)
pangaribawa influence
pangarsa leader
pangayoman shelter, sanctuary
panggilan dial
panginepan inn
pangiriman delivery
paningalan sight
panjang long
panjenengan you (*pron.*)
pantai beach, coast, shore
pantes proper (*adj.*)
panyadé daging butcher
panyerat author
panyuwun request
papan location, place; **papan kagem ngungsi** refuge; **papan palenggahan** seat; **papan panggenipun piyambak** private room; **papan tinggal** settlement; **papan wara-wara** information desk
parkir parking
parlemen parliament
pas exact; fit; fitting
pasal section
pasangan pair
pasien patient (*n.*)
pasir sand
paspor passport
pasrah surrender (*v.*)
pasta pasta
pasuryan face
patirasa painkiller
paugeran rule
paving pavement
pawarta news
pawiwahan wedding
pawiyatan education
pawon kitchen
payon roof
Pebruari February

pedhal pedal; **pedhal gas** accelerator (gas pedal); **pedhal kopling** clutch pedal
pedhes spicy
pedhut fog
pegawé employee
pegel painful
pegunungan mountain
pejah die; off (*adv.*/*adj.*)
peken marketplace; **peken swalayan** supermarket; **peken rombéngan** flea market
pelabuhan harbor
pelataran balcony
pemakaman funeral
pemandangan scenery
pemanggih view
pembalut wanita sanitary napkin
pembersih kering dry cleaner
pemburu hunter
pemilihan election
penatu laundromat
pendaftaran admission; registration
pendamelan job
pendingin udara/AC air conditioning
penduduk asli native
penerangan lighting
penerbangan flight
penerjemah translator
pengacara attorney, lawyer
pengadilan court
pengalaman experience
pengapian ignition
pengering dryer
pèngetan warning
penggalih think
pengganggu intruder
penggantos substitute
penghasilan income
penghuni occupant
pengobatan medication
pengungsi refugee
penjagi guard (*n.*); **penjagi toko** shopkeeper
penolak srangga insect repellant
penukaran mata uang currency exchange
penumpang passenger
penyiar announcer
peperangan war
perabotan furniture
pérak silver
perang battle (*n.*)
pérangan piece
perangko stamp
perawat nurse
perban bandage
percados trust
perhiasan jewelry
perih pain
perkémahan campground

permanen permanent (*adj.*)
permèn candy
peron platform
persen percent
perserikatan union
persimpangan junction
pertanian agriculture
pertelon intersection
perusahaan company
pesadéyan sale
pesagi square; **pesagi dawa** rectangle
pesen message, order
peso knife
pésta party
peta map; **peta margi** road map
peteng dark
pethak white
petugas officer
piano piano
pijet massage
pikantuk malih retrieve
pikir idea
piknik picnic
pil pill; **pil kagem saré** sleeping pill
pilek flu, influenza
pilihan option
pinanggih meet (*v.*)
pinarak layover
pingin want
pinjaman loan (*n.*)
pinten-pinten some
pipa pipe
pir peach
piramida pyramid
piranthi musik musical instrument
piranti equipment, kit, tool
piring plate
pisang banana
pit bicycle
pita ribbon
pitados believe
pitakèn question
pitakènan inquiry
pitik chicken
pitu seven
pitulas seventeen
pitulungan aid
pitung dasa seventy
piyama pajamas
piyambakan alone
piyambakipun (èstri) she; **piyambakipun (jalér)** he
plastik plastic
plesir trip
poin point
pojokan corner
polisi police
politik politics
polusi pollution
pon pound (*n.*)
pondokan hostel
popok kagem sepindhah diaper
poros axle

porselin pottery
pot pot
potlot pencil
prajurit soldier
prangko postage
prasasti monument
prau boat, ship
preinan vacation
prekawis case, issue, problem
présidèn president
pribadhi private
pribadi personal
printer printer
privasi privacy
priyantun someone
produk product; **produk susu** dairy
profesional professional
profesor professor
profil profile (*n.*)
promosi promotion
propinsi province
protes protest
Protestan Protestant
proyek project
psikolog psychologist
pucuk peak
pucuk tip
puding pudding
pulau island
punapa what; **punapa kémawon** anything; **punapa kémawon** any
pundhak shoulder
pundhut pick
pungkasan end, last
pungkasaning minggu weekend
punika it; that, this
punjering kitha downtown
pupu thigh
pusat center; **pusat belanja** shopping center

R

racikan finger
racun poison
radang usus buntu appendicitis
radhiyo radio
radin flat
ragbi rugby
ragi yeast
rah blood
raja pati murder
rajakaya animal
raket intimate
rakyat folk
rancang plan
randat late
rangkèt arrest (*v.*)
rangkulan hug
rangsum ration
ransel knapsack
ranté chain
raos flavor
rapat meeting

rasio ratio
rasukan clothing
rawuh arrive
Rebo Wednesday
reco statue
referensi reference
reged dirty
regi price, rate; **regi kamar** room rate
reguler regular
rejim regime
rekening bank bank account
rel rail; **rél sepur** railroad
relawan volunteer
rem brake (*n.*)
rematik arthritis
remen happy
rencana program
rèncang companion, friend, partner
rendheng spring (*season*)
répot busy
republik republic
reruntuhan ruins
resèp prescription
reservasi reservation
resik clean
resiko risk
resmi formal
resmi legal
resmi official
restoran restaurant
revolusi revolution
rewang maid
ribut noise
rikma hair
rina daytime, noon
ringkesan resume
risak broken
rodha wheel
rok skirt
romantis romantic
roti bread; **roti isi** sandwich; **roti kering** pastry; **roti tawar** loaf
royalti royalty
ruang bawah tanah basement
ruang konferènsi conference room
ruang makan dining room
ruang santai lounge
ruda peksa rape

S

saben every
sabuk pengaman seat belt
sabun soap; **sabun bubuk** detergent
sadel saddle
saé good, nice
saè great
saèstu most (*adv.*)
saged can (*modal v.*); able; **saged dipunbucal** disposable

sains science
sak pocket
sakdèrèngipun before (*prep.*)
sakiwatengenipun around
saklajengipun next, then (*adv.*)
sakmestinipun well (*interj.*)
saksampunipun after
sakumpulan population
sakwangsulipun opposite
sakwangsulipun reverse (*v.*)
salad salad
salah paham misunderstanding
salam greeting
salebeting inside; **salebeting ruangan** indoor
salju snow (*n.*)
salon salon
saluran channel
sambat complain
sami equal, same
samodra ocean
sampanye champagne
sampo shampoo
sampurna perfect
samudra sea
sandal sandals
sandera hostage
sanèsipun other
sanga nine
sangalas nineteen
sangang dasa ninety
sanget very (*adj.*)
santai casual
sapunika now
sarapan breakfast
saré asleep; sleep
sarem salt
sareng together
sarujuk agree
sasi month
satelit satellite
sawat throw
sawatawis temporary (*adj.*)
sawer snake
sawijining something
sayuran vegetable
scanner scanner
sebrang across
séda dead
sedanten all (*pron.*)
sedasa ten
sedaya entire
sedayanipun total
sedh èrèk èstri sister
sedih sad
segawon dog
seger fresh
segitiga triangle
sekar flower
sekawan four; **sekawan dasa** forty; **sekawan welas** fourteen
sekèco pleasant

sèket fifty
sekolah school
sekretaris secretary
seks sex
sekulèr secular (*adj.*)
séla stone
Selasa Tuesday
selé jam
selendang scarf
semèn cement
seminar seminar
semir dye
sèn cent
senat senate
senator senator
séndhok spoon
Senèn Monday
senggang spare (*adj.*)
seni art; **seni kerakyatan** folk art
senior senior
sensitif sensitive
sènter flashlight
sepalih half
sepata swear
sepatu shoe; **sepatu bot** boot; **sepatu es** skate
sepèdha montor motorcycle
sepen quiet
sepindhah first, once
seprapat quarter
seprei bedding, sheet
September September
sepuh old
sepur train; **sepur cepet** express train
serangan assault, attack; **serangan jantung** heart attack
serat letter, mail; **serat kabar** newspaper
serbèt napkin
séréal cereal
server server
sesrawungan communication
setèlan suit
Setu Saturday
setunggal one; **setunggal arah** one-way
sewelas eleven
sewidhak sixty
sewu thousand
sidang trial
sigarèt cigarette
sikat waja toothbrush
silèt razor
SIM driver's license
simbol symbol
sinagog synagogue
sinar x x-ray
sinau learn, study
singsot whistle (*v.*)
sinten who (*pron.*); anybody; **sinten kémawon** anyone; **sinten sinyal** signal
sipat nature
siram bath; bathe
sirine siren
sisih side

sistem system
siswa student
siti ground, land
siyaga ready
ski ski
slamet safe
slorokan drawer; locker
soca eye
sogok bribe
sonten afternoon; evening
sop soup
sora loud
sorak shout
sosis sausage
speedometer speedometer
sragam uniform
srangga insect
srengéngé sun
stadion stadium
staf staff
standar standard (*n.*)
stasiun station; **stasiun metro** metro station; **stasiun sepur** train station
steril sterile
stok supplies
suanten sound
suci holy
suhu temperature
suket grass
suku foot; leg; tribe; **suku cadang** spare part
sulistya beautiful
sumadya available
sumber source
sumeh hospitality
supé forget
surung push
susu milk
suwiwi wing
swalayan self-service
swanten voice
syair poem
syaraf nerve

T

tabuh hour
tagian bill
takeran (0,568 liter) pint
taksi cab, taxi
tali rope
talingan ear
taman park
tambang mine
tampon tampon
tamu guest
tanda sign
tanggal date; **tanggal kadaluarsa** expiration date; **tanggal lair** date of birth
tanggi neighbor
tanggon reliable
tangki gas gas tank
tanglet ask

tanpa without
tapak trail; **tapak asma** signature; **tapak suku** footpath
tarif fare
tas bag; **tas geger** backpack
tata basa grammar
tatahan sculpture
tatu hurt
tatu injury; sore (*adj.*)
taun kepengker last year
taun ngajeng next year
taunan annual
tawanan prisoner
tawon bee
tebih away
tebih far
tèh tea
telas exhaust
televisi television
tèlepon telephone, phone; **tèlepon genggem** mobile phone; **tèlepon umum** public telephone
tembang song
témbok wall
tembung word; **tembung kriya** verb
tenanan serious
téndha tent
tengah middle, medium (*adj.*); **tengah dalu** midnight
tenggat waktu deadline
tenggorokan throat
tengkorak skull
tentara army
tentrem peace
tepang recognize
terminal bis bus terminal
ternak cattle
teroris terrorist
tersangka suspect (*n.*)
tès test
tetandhuran plant
tetanèn farm
tiga three
tigan egg
tigang dasa thirty
tikèt ticket; **tikèt minggah kendaraan** boarding pass
tikus mouse, rat
tilas route
tindak go, leave
tindakan travel
tindhak-kondur round-trip
tingkat level
tipis thin
tisu bayi baby wipes
tisu pakiwan toilet paper
titik pepanggihan checkpoint
tiyang people, person; **tiyang cacat** handi-capped; **tiyang Éropa**

European; **tiyang jaler** man; **tiyang manca** stranger; **tiyang mlampah** pedestrian; **tiyang ngemis** beggar; **tiyang sepuh** parent
tlaga lake
tlatah area, region
Tn. Mr. (*title*)
toko shop, store; **toko buku** bookstore; **toko klonthong** grocery store; **toko rongsokan** secondhand store; **toko roti** bakery
tomat tomato
tombol button
tong barrel
tontonan entertainment
topi hat
toserba convenience store; department store
toya water
tradisi tradition
tradisional traditional
transfer transfer
transmisi otomatis automatic transmission
transplantasi transplant
transportasi transportation
trek truck
tresna love
troli trolley
trowongan tunnel
tuan sir
tujuan destination, purpose
tukang cukur barber
tukang ramal fortune-teller
tuladha example
tuladha sample
tuma flea; lice
tumindhak act (*v.*)
tumut follow; share
tunawisma homeless
tundha delay
tunggal single (*adj.*)
tuntutan demand (*n.*)
turangga horse
turis tourist
tutuk mouth
tutup lid

U

udara air
ugel-ugel ankle; wrist
ugi also
ukara sentence
ukiran engraving
ukum law
ukuran measure, size
ulam fish
umum general, public
unggah-ungguh courtesy

unggas poultry
ungu purple
universitas university
unjukan beverage
unjukan drink (*n.*)
untung lucky
unus puncture
upah salary
urubing geni flare
usap wipe
utama main (*adj.*)
utang debt
utawi or
uwos rice

V

vaksinasi vaccinate
vanila vanilla
vegetarian vegetarian
vidio video
virus virus
visa visa; **visa mlebet** entry visa

W

wadi secret
waja tooth
wajib mandatory
walikota mayor
wana forest, jungle
wanara monkey
wanci siang midday
wangsul return (*v.*)
wanita woman
wara-wara announcement; information
warga negara citizen; civilian
warsa year; **Warsa énggal** New Year
wartawan reporter
wasit referee (*n.*)
waspadha beware
was-was worry (*v.*)
wates barrier; border; **wates cepet** speed limit
watuk cough
wc umum public toilet
wekdal saklajengipun future
wekdhal time
werni color; **werni cokelat** brown
wesi iron
wétan east
wewangunan building
wèwèh gift
wicanten talk
wilayah territory
wingking rear
wingkingipun behind
winih seed
wiraga musician
wiwitan beginning
wiwitan early
woh ara fig
woh-wohan fruit

wol wool
wolu eight
wolulas eighteen
wolung dasa eighty
wonten ngandhap below
wonten ngandhapipun siti underground (*adj./adv.*)
wonten nginggil over (*prep.*)
wonten ngriki here, there
wonten njawi outside
wonten pundi where (*adv.*); **wonten pundi kémawon** anywhere
wortel carrot
wudha naked
wulan moon
wungu wake
wuta blind

Y

Yahudi Jew
yogurt yogurt
yuswa age
yuta million

Z

zaitun olive

ENGLISH-JAVANESE DICTIONARY

A

able saged
about ngéngingi
above ing nginggil
academy akademi
accelerator (*gas pedal*) pedal gas
accent aksèn/logat
accept nampi
access (*n.*) margi mlebet
accident katiwasan
accommodations akomodasi
account akun
accountant akuntan
accurate akurat
accuse nuduh
acre (*0.4 hectares*) are (0,4 hektar)
across sebrang
act (*v.*) tumindhak
activist aktivis
activity kagiyatan
actor aktor
actual aktual
add nambah
address (*n.*) alamat
administration administrasi
admission pendaftaran
admit ndaftaraken
adult diwasa
advertisement iklan
afraid ajrih
after saksampunipun
afternoon sonten
again malih
against nglawan
age yuswa
agency (*n.*) agensi
agent agen
agree sarujuk
agriculture pertanian
aid pitulungan
AIDS AIDS
air udara
air conditioning (AC) pendingin udara (AC)
airline maskapai
airplane montor mabur
airport bandara; **airport tax** pajek bandara
aisle gang
alarm alarm
alcohol alkohol
alive gesang
all (*pron.*) sedanten
allergy alergi
alley gang alit
allow marengaken
allowed dipun parengaken
almond almon
alone piyambakan
also ugi
altar (*n.*) altar
altitude kainggilan
aluminum foil kertas alumunium
always (*adv.*) asring
ambassador duta besar

ambulance ambulan
amenities fasilitas
among ing antawisipun
amount (*n.*) gunggung
and kaliyan
anemic anemia
anesthetic obat bius
angry duka
animal rajakaya
ankle ugel-ugel
anniversary ambal warsa
announcement wara-wara
announcer penyiar
annual taunan
antibiotics antibiotik
antifreeze anti beku
antique antik
antiseptic anti septik
any punapa kémawon
anybody sinten
anyone sinten kémawon
anything punapa kémawon
anywhere wonten pundi kémawon
apartment apartemèn
apologize nyuwun pangapunten
appeal narik
appear ketingal
appendicitis radang usus buntu
appetite nepsu dhahar
apple apel
appointment janji
apricot aprikot
April April
architecture arsitèktur
area tlatah
argue padudon
arm lengen
army tentara
around sakiwaten-genipun
arrest (*v.*) rangkèt
arrive rawuh
art seni
arthritis rematik
ash lebu
ask tanglet
asleep saré
aspirin aspirin
assault serangan
assist mbiyantu
associate (*n.*) kanca
asthma asma
ATM ATM
attack serangan
attorney pengacara
August Agustus
author panyerat
automatic otomatis
automatic transmission transmisi otomatis
automobile montor
autumn musim gugur
available sumadya
avenue margi ageng
avoid ngindari
awake nglilir

away tebih
axle poros

B

baby bayi; **baby wipes** tisu bayi
babysitter pamomong bayi
back geger
backpack tas geger
bad awon
bag tas
baggage koper; **baggage check** mirsani gawanan
bakery toko roti
balcony pelataran
ball bal
banana pisang
bandage perban
bank bank; **bank account** rekening bank
bar bar
barber tukang cukur
barrel tong
barrier wates
base dasar
basement ruang bawah tanah
basin mangkok
basket kranjang
basketball bal basket
bat lawa
bath siram; **bath towel** anduk kagem siram
bathe siram
bathing suit ageman siram
bathroom padusan
battery baterai
battle (*n.*) perang
be (*v.*, **am, is, are, was, were, been**) inggih punika
beach pantai
bean kacang polong
beautiful sulistya
because of amargi
become (*v.*) dados
bed dipan
bedding seprei
bedroom kamar
bee tawon
beef daging sapi
beer bir
before (*prep.*) sakdèrèngipun
beggar tiyang ngemis
beginning wiwitan
behind wingkingipun
believe pitados
bell bèl
below wonten ngandhap
berry berri
beverage unjukan
beware waspadha
bible injil
bicycle pit
big ageng
bill tagian

birth certificate akte klairan
birthday ambal warsa
bite cokot
bitter pait
black cemeng
blanket kemul
bleed medal rahipun
bless berkah
blind wuta
blister mlepuh
blood rah; **blood type** golongan darah
blue biru
boarding pass tiket minggah kendaraan
boat prau
body awak
bomb bom
bone balung
bonus bonus
book buku
bookstore toko buku
boot sepatu bot
border wates
bottle botol
bottom (*n.*) ngandhap
box (*n.*) kotak; (*v.*) nglebetaken wontenkotak
boy laré jaler
boyfriend kanca jaler raket
brake (*n.*) rem
bread roti
break (*v.*) ngrisak
breakfast sarapan
breathe ambegan
bribe sogok
brick bata
bridge kreteg
bring mbeta
broken risak
brother kang mas
brown werni cokelat
building wewangunan
bull banthèng
bullet mimis
bureaucracy birokrasi
bury mendhem
bus bis; **bus terminal** terminal bis
business bisnis
busy répot
but (*conj.*) nanging
butcher panyadé daging
butter mentèga
button tombol
buy mundhut

C

cab taksi
cabinet lemari kaca
cable kabel
cable TV kabel TV
cafe kafé
cage kandhang
cake jajanan
calendar kalènder
call (*v.*) nimbali

camera kamèra
camp kémah
campground perkémahan
can (*modal v.*) saged
cancel batal
candy permèn
car mobil
card kertu
carpet karpèt
carrot wortel
carry ngasta
carry-on nglajengaken
cart kerèta
case prekawis
cash (*v.*) mbayar tunai; (*n.*) arta tunai
casual santai
cat kucing
catch (*v.*) nyepeng
cathedral katedral
cattle ternak
cave guwo
CD CD
cement semèn
cemetery makam
cent sèn
center pusat
century abad
cereal séréal
chain ranté
chair dingklik
champagne sampanye
change (*v.*) ngganti; (*n.*) ganti
changing room kamar gantos
channel saluran
chapel greja alit
chapter babagan
charge (*n.*) béaya
cheap mirah
check (*v.*) mriksa; (*n.*) cek; **check in** check in; **check out** check out
checkpoint titik pepanggihan
cheese kèju
chef koki
chemical kimia
chew mamah
chicken pitik
chickpeas kacang dawa
chief (*adj.*) mandhégani
child laré
childcare ngupakara laré
chocolate coklat
choke nyekik
church gréja
cigarette sigarèt
cinema bioskop
cinnamon kayu manis
circle bunder
citizen warga negara
city kitha
civilian warga negara
clap keplok
class kelas
classic klasik

clean resik
client langganan
cliff jurang
climate mangsa
climb minggah
clinic klinik
clock jam
close (*adv.*) caket; (*v.*) nutup
closed katutup
cloth kain
clothing rasukan
club klub
clutch pedal pedhal kopling
coast pantai
coat mantel
cocoa kokoa
coconut krambil
coffee kopi
coin koin
cold asrep
collect ngempalaken
color werni
comb jungkat
come dumugi
comedy lelucon
comfortable krasan
commission komisi
communication sesrawungan
companion rèncang
company perusahaan
compare mbandingaken
compensation kompensasi
complain sambat
complicated ewet
compromise kompromi
computer komputer
conceal ndelikaken
concert konsèr
concrete beton
concussion gegar otak
condom kondom
conductor kernèt
conference konferènsi; **conference room** ruang konferènsi
confirm genah
constipated bebelen
constitution konstitusi
consulate konsulat
consult konsultasi
contagious nular
contraception kontrasèpsi
contraceptive kontrasèptip
contract kontrak
convenience store toserba
convenient nyaman
cook masak
copy jiplakan
cord kabel
corn jagung
corner pojokan
correct (*adj.*) leres
corrupt korup
cosmetics kosmètik
cost bèaya

cotton katun
cough watuk
country negari; **country code** kode negari
court pengadilan
courtesy unggah-ungguh
cover nutupi
cover charge bèaya mlebet
cream krim
credit krédit; **credit card** kertu krédit
crime kadurjanan
crowd keraméan
crutches kruk
cry nangis
culture budhaya
cup cangkir
cure (*n.*) jampi
curfew jam malam
currency mata uang; **currency exchange** penukaran mata uang
customer langganan
customs béa cukai; **customs declaration** formulir béa cukai
cut motong

D

dairy produk susu
damage kerisakan
dance beksa
danger bebaya
dark peteng
date tanggal
date of birth tanggal lair
daughter laré èstri
dawn pajar
day dinten
daytime rina
dead séda
deadline tenggat waktu
deaf budheg
debt utang
decade dékade
December Désember
decide mutusaken
decision kaputusan
deck dhèk
declare nyatakaken
deep jero
delay tundha
delicious éca
deliver ngirim
delivery pangiriman
demand (*n.*) tuntutan
democracy démokrasi
dentist dokter gigi
deny mbantah
deodorant déodoran
department store toserba
departure budhal
deposit deposito
depot depot
desert padhang pasir
desk méja

dessert dhaharan panutup
destination tujuan
detergent sabun bubuk
detour jalan lingkar
diabetic kencing manis
diagnosis diagnosa
dial panggilan
dialing code kode panggilan
diaper popok kagem sepindhah
diarrhea diare
dictate ndikté
dictionary kamus
die pejah
diesel disel
different bènten
difficult èwet
dine dhaharan dalu
dining room ruang makan
dinner dhahar dalu
diplomat diplomat
direction(s) ener
directory direktori; **directory assistance** bantuan arah
dirt larahan
dirty reged
disability cacat
disabled cacat
disagree mboten sarujuk
disaster bebaya
discount diskon
disease lelara
dish dhaharan
disposable saged dipunbucal
dispute (*v.*) mbantah
district distrik
disturb ngganggu
dive nyilem
dizzy mumet
do nglampahi
dock dok
doctor dokter
document dokumèn
dog segawon
dollar dolar
domestic domestik
door lawang
double dobel
dough jladrènan
down dawah
downtown punjering kitha
dozen dosin
drain nguras
drama drama
drawer slorokan
dress (*n.*) gaun; (*v.*) dandan
drink (*n.*) unjukan; (*v.*) ngunjuk
drive nyetir
driver's license SIM
drown kèrem
drowsy ngantuk
drug obat
drugstore apotik
drunk mendem

dry (*adj.*) garing; (*v.*) nggaringaken
dry cleaner pembersih kering
dryer pengering
dust (*v.*) ngelap lebu
duty-free bebas pajek
DVD DVD
dye semir

E

ear talingan
earache gerah talingan
early wiwitan
earth bumi
earthquake lindhu
east wétan
eat dhahar
economy ekonomi
education pawiyatan
egg tigan
eight wolu
eighteen wolulas
eighty wolung dasa
election pemilihan
electric kelistrikan
electricity listrik
elevator lift
eleven sewelas
e-mail email
embassy kedutaan
emergency darurat
employee pegawé
employer majikan
empty kothong
end pungkasan
enemy mungsuh
energy kakuwatan
engine mesin
engineer insinyur
English language basa Inggris
engraving ukiran
enough cekap
enter mlebet
entertainment tontonan
entire sedaya
entrance margi mlebet
entry entri; **entry visa** visa mlebet
envelope amplop
epileptic epilepsi
equal sami
equipment piranti
escalator eskalator
estimate nginten-inten
ethnic etnis
Europe Éropa
European tiyang Éropa
evacuate dipun ungsiaken
even adil
evening sonten
event kadadosan
eventually ènggal-ènggal
ever naté
every saben
exact pas
examine mriksa

example tuladha
except kejawi
excess langkung
exchange gantos; **exchange rate** nilai tukar
exclude mboten kalebet
exhaust telas
exhibit (*v.*) nedahaken
exit medal
expense blanja
expensive awis
experience pengalaman
expiration date tanggal kadaluarsa
explain njlèntrèhaken
export ngèkspor
express cepet; **express train** sepur cepet
extra ekstra
eye soca
eyeglasses kacatingal

F

fabric kain
face pasuryan
fall dhawah
false (*adj.*) lepat
family kulawarga
far tebih
fare tarif
farm tetanèn
fast food dhaharan cepet saji
fat lemak
father bapak
faucet kran
fax (*n.*) faksimili
February Pebruari
fee beaya
feel ngraos
female èstri
fence pager
ferry kapal fèri
festival festival
fever mriang
field lapangan
fifteen gangsal welas
fifty sèket
fig woh ara
fill ngisi
film film
find kepanggih
finger racikan
fire geni; **fire alarm** alarm kebakaran
firewood kajeng bakar
fireworks kembang api
first sepindah
first-aid kit P3K
first-class kelas setunggal
fish ulam
fisherman nelayan
fishing mancing; **fishing license** ijin mancing; **fishing permitted** angsal mancing; **fishing rod** gagang pancing

fist gegeman
fit pas
fitting pas; **fitting room** kamar pas
five gangsal
fix ndandosi
flag gendéra
flame murub
flare urubing geni
flash kilat; **flash photography** lampu kilat fotografi
flashlight sènter
flat radin; **flat tire** ban bocor
flavor raos
flea tuma; **flea market** peken rombéngan
flight penerbangan; **flight number** nomer penerbangan
flood banjir
floor jogan
flour glepung
flourish ngapik-apik
flower sekar
flu pilek
fluent lancar
fluid mbanyu
flush mbilas
fly mabur
fog pedhut
folk rakyat; **folk art** seni kerakyatan
follow tumut
food dhaharan; **food poisoning** keracunan dhaharan
foot suku
football (soccer) bal-balan
footpath tapak suku
forehead palarapan
foreign manca; **foreign currency** mata uang manca; **foreign languages** basa manca
forest wana
forget supé
forgive ngapura
fork garpu
formal resmi
fortune beja
fortune-teller tukang ramal
forty sekawan dasa
fountain air mancur
four sekawan
fourteen sekawan welas
fraud palsu
free bèbas
freeze ndamel beku
fresh seger
Friday Jumuah
friend rèncang
front ngajeng; **front desk** meja ngajeng
frozen beku
fruit woh-wohan
fry nggorèng
fuel bahan bakar

full kebak
fun nyenengken
funeral pemakaman
furnished dipun lengkapi
furniture perabotan
future wekdal saklajengipun

G

game dolanan
garden (*n.*) kebon
gas tank tangki gas
gasoline bènsin
gear gir
general umum
get angsal
gift wèwèh
girl kenya
girlfriend pacar èstri
give maringi
glass gelas
glasses (eye) kaca tingal
glue lèm
go tindak
goat mèndha
gold emas
good saé
goods barang-barang
government pamarèntah
gram gram
grammar tata basa
grandfather èyang kakung
grandmother èyang putri
grape anggur
grass suket
great saè
green ijem
greeting salam
grocery store toko klonthong
ground (*n.*) siti
group kempalan
guard (*n.*) penjagi
guest tamu
guide (*n.*) panduan
guidebook buku panduan
guilty lepat
gun bedhil
gym gym

H

hair rikma
half sepalih
hall aula
halt mandheg
hand asta
handicapped tiyang cacat
happy remen
harbor pelabuhan
hard atos
harm mbebayani
hat topi
hazard bebaya
he piyambakipun (jalér)

head mustaka
health kesehatan; **health insurance** asuransi kesehatan
hear mireng
heart jantung; **heart attack** serangan jantung
heat bentèr
heavy awrat
hello halo
help mbiyantu
herb jampi
here wonten ngriki
heterosexual heteroseksual
hey (*interj.*) hei
highway jalan tol
hike minggah
hill gunung alit
HIV HIV
hole bolongan
holiday liburan
holy suci
home griya
homeless tunawisma
homosexual homoseksual
honest jujur
honey madu
honeymoon bulan madu
horse turangga
hospital griya sakit
hospitality sumeh
hostage sandera
hostel pondokan
hostile mungsuhan
hot bentèr
hotel hotel
hour tabuh
house griya
how kadospundi
hug rangkulan
human manungsa; **human rights** (*n.*) hak asasi manungsa
hundred atusan
hungry luwé
hunt berburu
hunter pemburu
hurry énggal-énggal
hurt tatu
husband garwa kakung

I

I kula
ice es
ID card KTP
idea pikir
identification identifikasi
identify ngidentifikasi
idiom idiom
if menawi
ignition pengapian
ignore ngrèmèhaken
illegal nglanggar
illness gerah
immigrant imigran
immigration imigrasi

impolite mboten sopan
import impor
income penghasilan
incorrect lepat
individual individual
indoor salebeting ruangan
inexpensive mirah
infant laré bayi
infect nginfeksi
infected kenging infeksi
infection infeksi
influence pangaribawa
influenza pilek
information wara-wara; **information desk** papan wara-wara
infrastructure infrastruktur
inject nyunthik
injury tatu
ink mangsi
inn panginepan
innocent mboten lepat
inquiry pitakènan
insect srangga; **insect bite** cokotan srangga; **insect repellant** penolak srangga
inside salebeting
inspect nginspeksi
instant instan
institution lembaga
insufficient mboten cekap
insulin insulin
insult ngina
insurance asuransi
international internasional
Internet internet
interpret nerjemahaken
interpretation interpretasi
interpreter juru basa
intersection pertelon
intimate raket
introduce oneself nepangaken piyambak
intruder pengganggu
invite ngundang
iron wesi
irritate nyababaken gatel
island pulau
issue prekawis
it punika
itch gatel
item barang
itinerary jadwal

J

jacket jaket
jail kunjara
jam selé
January Januari
jar blèk
jeans clana jins
Jew Yahudi
jewelry perhiasan

job pendamelan
join ndèrèk
journalist jurnalis
judge hakim
jug kendhi
juice jus
July Juli
jump mlumpat
jumper cables kabel jumper
junction persimpangan
June Juni
jungle wana
just namung
justice kaadilan

K

keep (*v.*) nyimpen
kettle kètèl
key kunci
kick nendhang
kid laré
kidnap nyulik
kidney ginjel
kill mejahi
kilogram kilogram
kilometer kilometer
kind macem
kiss ngambung
kit piranti
kitchen pawon
knapsack ransel
knee dengkul
knife peso
knit ngrajut
knock ngethuk
knot bundel
know mangertos
kosher kosher

L

lady èstri
lake tlaga
lamb mendo
lamp diyan
land siti
lane jalur
language basa
laptop leptop
large ageng
last pungkasan; **last year** taun kepengker
late randat
later mangké
laugh gujeng
laundromat penatu
laundry kumbahan
lavatory jamban
law ukum
lawyer pengacara
layover pinarak
leader pangarsa
league liga
learn sinau
leather kulit
leave tindak
left ninggalaken
leg suku

legal resmi
legislature DPR
lemon jeruk lemon
lens lensa
less (*adv*., little) kirang
letter serat
lettuce kol
level tingkat
library kapustakan
lice tuma
license ijin
lid tutup
lie cidra
life gesang
lift njunjung
light cahya
lighting penerangan
like (*v.*) nyenengi
lime jeruk limau
limit (*v.*) maringi wates
lip lathi
liquid èncèr
liquor minuman keras
list daptar
listen mirengaken
liter liter
litter larahan
little (*adj.*) alit
live (*v.*) gesang
liver manah
lizard kadal
load (*v.*) ngemat
loaf roti tawar
loan (*n.*) pinjaman
lobby lobi
local lokal
location papan
lock ngunci; **lock out** ngurung
locker slorokan
long panjang
look mirsani
loose kendo
lose kalah
lost ical
loud sora
lounge ruang santai
love tresna
low andhap
lucky untung
luggage bagasi
lunch dhahar siyang

M

machine mesin
mad (*adj.*) édan
maid rewang
mail (*n.*) serat; (*v.*) ngirimaken serat
main (*adj.*) utama
make (*v.*) ndamel
man tiyang jaler
mandatory wajib
manual (*n.*) manual
many kathah
map peta
marketplace peken
marriage nikah
married krama
marry krama

massage pijet,mijet
math matematika
mattress kasur
maximum maksimal
mayor walikota
meal dhaharan
measure ukuran
meat daging
mechanic mekanik
medication pengobatan
medicine jampi
medium (*adj.*) tengah
meet (*v.*) pinanggih
meeting rapat
melon melon
melt mbanyu
member anggota
menstruation haid
mental méntal
menu menu
message pesen
messenger caraka
metal logam
meter meter
metro station stasiun metro
microwave mikrowave
midday wanci siang
middle tengah
midnight tengah dalu
might menawi
migraine migren
mild (*adj.*) alus
mile mil
military militer
milk susu
million yuta
mine tambang
minimum minimal
minor (*adj.*) minor
mint mint
minute menit
mirror kaca
misunderstanding salah paham
mix campuran
mobile phone telepon genggem
moment nalika
Monday Senèn
money arta
monkey wanara
month sasi
monument prasasti
moon wulan
more (*adv.*) langkung
morning enjing
mosque mesjid
mosquito lemut; **mosquito net** klambu
most (*adv.*) saèstu
motel motèl
mother ibu
mother-in-law ibu marasepuh
motion sickness mabuk
motor montor
motorcycle sepèdha montor
mount giri
mountain pegunungan
mouse tikus

moustache bréngos
mouth tutuk
move (*v.*) mindhahaken
movie film; **movie theater** bioskop
Mr. (*title*) Tn.
Mrs. (*title*) Ny.
Ms. (*title*) Nn.
much (*adv.*) kathah
mud endut
mural gegambar wontentembok
murder raja pati
muscle otot
museum museum
mushroom jamur
music musik
musical instrument piranthi musik
musician wiraga
Muslim Muslim
mussels kerang
mystery misteri

N

naked wudha
name asma
napkin serbèt
narrow ciut
nation bangsa
native penduduk asli
nature sipat
nausea mules
navigation navigasi
navy angkatan laut
near (*prep.*) celak
nearby (*adj.*) celak
neck jangga
necklace kalung
need (*v.*) mbetahaken
needle dom
neighbor tanggi
neighborhood lingkungan
nephew keponakan jaler
nerve syaraf
neutral (*adj.*) netral
never mboten nate
new (*adj.*) énggal; **New Year** Warsa énggal; **New Year's Day** Dinten Warsa Énggal; **New Year's Eve** Malem Warsa énggal
news pawarta
newspaper serat kabar
next saklajengipun; **next to** celak kaliyan; **next year** taun ngajeng
nice saé
niece keponakan èstri
night dalu
nightlife kehidupan malam
nine sanga
nineteen sangalas
ninety sangang dasa
no mboten
noise ribut

non-smoking mboten ngeses
noodles mie
noon rina
normal normal
north lèr
northeast lèr wétan
northwest lèr kilèn
nose grana
note cathetan
nothing mboten wonten
November Nopember
now sapunika
nowhere (*adv.*) mboten wonten pundi-pundi
nuclear (*adj.*) nuklir
number nomer
nun biarawati
nurse perawat
nuts kacang

O

occupant penghuni
occupation pakaryan
ocean samodra
o'clock jam
October Oktober
octopus gurita
odor ambet
off (*adv./adj.*) pejah
offend nyinggung manah
office kantor
officer petugas
official resmi
often asring
oil oli
OK inggih
old sepuh
olive zaitun
on amurub
once sepindhah
one setunggal
one-way setunggal arah
onion bawang pethak
only namung
open mbikak
opera opera
operator juru ladhèn
opposite sakwangsulipun
option pilihan
or utawi
oral lisan
orange oranye
orchard kebon woh-wohan
orchestra orkestra
order pesen
ordinary biasa
organ organ
organic organik
original asli
other sanèsipun
ought kedahipun
our awakipun piyambak
out (*adv.*) medal
outdoor (*adj.*) njawi ruangan
outside wonten njawi
oven oven
over (*prep.*) wonten nginggil

overdose kaluwihan dosis
overnight kala dalu
own (*v.*) nggadhahi
owner (*n.*) ingkang kagungan
oxygen oksigen

P

pack mbungkus
package pakèt
page kaca
paid mbayar
pain perih
painful pegel
painkiller patirasa
pair pasangan
pajamas piyama
pan panci
pants clana
paper dluwang
parcel bingkisan
pardon (*n.*) pangapunten
parent tiyang sepuh
park taman
parking parkir
parliament parlemen
partner rèncang
party pésta
passenger penumpang
passport paspor
password kata sandi
pasta pasta
pastry roti kering
path jalur
patience kesabaran
patient (*n.*) pasien
pavement paving
pay mbayar
payment gajian
pea kacang polong
peace tentrem
peach pir
peak pucuk
peanuts kacang tanah
pedal pedhal
pedestrian tiyang mlampah
pen bolpèn
penalty denda
pencil potlot
people tiyang
pepper mrica
percent persen
perfect sampurna
period nalika
permanent (*adj.*) permanen
permission ijin
permit (*v.*) ngijinaken; (*n.*) ijin
person tiyang
personal pribadi
pest hama
pet ingon-ingon
petrol bènsin
pharmacy farmasi
phone tèlpon; **phone booth** kotak tèlpon; **phone card** kertu

tèlpon; **phone number** nomer tèlpon
photograph foto
phrase frasa
physician dokter
piano piano
pick pundhut
picnic piknik
picture gambar
pie pai
piece pérangan
pig babi
pigeon manuk dara
pill pil
pillow bantal
pint takeran 0,568 liter
pipe pipa
place papan
plan rancang
plane montor mabur
plant tetandhuran
plastic plastik
plate piring
platform peron
play (*n.*) pagelaran; (*v.*) dolanan
pleasant sekèco
please nuwun sewu
plug nyolokaken
pocket sak
poem syair
point poin
poison racun
police polisi; **police station** kantor polisi
polite sopan santun
politics politik
pollution polusi
pool kolam renang
population sakumpulan
pork daging cèlèng
portable (*adj.*) gampil dibeta
possibly (*adv.*) menawi
post office kantor pos
postage prangko
postal code kode pos
postbox kotak pos
postcard kertu pos
postpone nundha
pot pot
potato kenthang
pottery porselin
poultry unggas
pound (*n.*) pon
pour nyuntak
poverty kemlaratan
power kekiatan
pray dedonga
prefer langkung remen
pregnant ngandhut
prescription resèp
president présidèn
price regi
priest pandhita
printer printer
prison kunjara
prisoner tawanan
privacy privasi
private pribadhi; **private property** kagunganipun

piyambak; **private room** papan panggenipun piyambak
prize hadhiah
probably menawi
problem prekawis
product (*n.*) produk
professional profesional
professor profesor
profile (*n.*) profil
profit bathi
program rencana
prohibit nglarang
project proyek
promise (*v.*) ndamel janji
promotion promosi
pronounce (*v.*) ngaturaken
proper (*adj.*) pantes
property kagungan
prosecute nuntut
protect ngayomi
protest protes
Protestant Protestan
province propinsi
psychologist psikolog
public umum; **public telephone** tèlpon umum; **public toilet** wc umum; **public transportation** angkutan umum
pudding puding
pull narik
pulse nadi
pump kompa
punch njotos
puncture unus
punish ngukum
purchase mundhut
pure asli
purple ungu
purpose tujuan
purse dompèt
push surung
puzzle cangkriman
pyramid piramida

Q

qualify kagungan kualitas
quality kualitas
quantity kuantitas
quarantine karantina
quarter seprapat
question pitakèn
queue antri
quick cepet
quiet sepen

R

radio radhiyo
rail rel
railroad rél sepur
rain jawah
ramp margi landai
rape ruda peksa
rapid cepet

rare jarang
rat tikus
rate regi
ratio rasio
ration rangsum
raw mentah
razor silèt
read maos
ready siyaga
rear wingking
reason alesanipun
reasonable masuk akal
rebel brontak
rebellion kraman
receipt kwitansi
receive nampi
recognize tepang
recommend nyaranaken
record ngrekam
rectangle pesagi dawa
recycle dipun olah malih
red abrit
referee (*n.*) wasit
reference referensi
refrigerator kulkas
refuge papan kagem ngungsi
refugee pengungsi
refund mbalèaken arta
regime rejim
region tlatah
registration pendaftaran
regular reguler
relationship gegayutan
relative mboten pasti
reliable tanggon
religion agami
remedy jampi
remember éling
remind ngélingaken
remove nyingkiraken
rent nyéwa
repair ndandosi; **repair shop** bengkel
repay mbayar malih
repeat ngambali
replace nggantos
reply jawab
report ngaturi pirsa
reporter wartawan
republic republik
request panyuwun
require mbetahaken
rescue nylametaken
reservation reservasi
reserve nyimpen
reservoir bendungan
respect hormat
rest istirahat
restaurant restoran
restricted (*adj.*) kawates
resume ringkesan
retrieve pikantuk malih
return (*v.*) wangsul
reverse (*v.*) sakwangsulipun
revive nyadaraken
revolution revolusi
rib iga
ribbon pita

rice uwos
ride nitih
right (*direction*) kanan
ring ali-ali
riot ontran-ontran
rip nyuwèk
risk resiko
river lèpèn
road margi; **road map** peta margi
roasted digarang
rob ngrampok
rock (*n.*) padhas
romance katresnan
romantic romantis
roof payon
room kamar; **room rate** regi kamar; **room service** layanan kamar
rope tali
rot (*v.*) mambu banger
rotten bosok
rough kasar
round-trip tindhak-kondur; **round-trip ticket** karcis tindhak-kondur
route tilas
royalty royalti
rubber karèt
rude kasar
rug karpèt
rugby ragbi
ruins reruntuhan
rule paugeran
run mlajeng

S

sacred kramat
sad sedih
saddle sadel
safe slamet
safety kaslametan
sail layar
salad salad
salary upah
sale pesadéyan
sales receipt nota pesadéyan
sales tax pajek penjualan
salon salon
salt sarem
same sami
sample tuladha
sanction denda
sanctuary pangayoman
sand pasir
sandals sandal
sandwich roti isi
sanitary napkin pembalut wanita
satellite satelit
Saturday Setu
sauce caos
sausage sosis
save nyinggahaken
saw graji
say ngendhika
scanner scanner
scar korèng
scarf selendang
scary medèni

scene adegan
scenery pemandangan
schedule jadual
school sekolah
science sains
scissors gunting
score biji
screen layar
screw baut
screwdriver obéng
sculpture tatahan
sea samudra
seafood dhaharan laut
search (*n.*) padosan
seasick mabuk laut
season musim
seasonal musiman
seat papan palenggahan; **seat belt** sabuk pengaman; **seat number** nomer kursi
second bekas
secondhand store toko rongsokan
secret wadi
secretary sekretaris
section pasal
secular sekulèr
security katentreman
sedative obat penenang
see ningali
seed winih
seek madosi
seem (*v.*) katingal
select (*v.*) milih
selection pamilih
self-service swalayan
sell nyadé
seminar seminar
senate senat
senator senator
send ngirimaken
senior senior
sensitive sensitif
sentence ukara
separate (*adj.*) kapisah; (*v.*) misahaken
September September
serious tenanan
servant juru ladèn
serve ladèn
server server
service ngladèni
settlement papan tinggal
seven pitu
seventeen pitulas
seventy pitung dasa
sew njahit
sex seks
shampoo sampo
share tumut
shark hiu
sharp landhep
shave nyukur
shaving cream krim cukur
she piyambakipun (èstri)
sheep méndha
sheet seprèi
shellfish kerang
shelter (*n.*) pangayoman

ship prau
shirt ageman
shoe sepatu
shoot (*v.*) némbak
shop toko
shopkeeper penjagi toko
shoplifting ngutil
shopping basket keranjang blanja
shopping center pusat belanja
shore (*n.*) pantai
short cendhèk
shot nembak
shoulder pundhak
shout sorak
show maringi pirsa
shower pancuran, grojogan
shut nutup
sick gerah
side sisih
sight paningalan
sightseeing ningali
sign tanda
signal sinyal
signature tapak asma
silver pérak
sing nembang
single (*n.*) bujang; (*adj.*) tunggal
sink klelep
sir tuan
siren sirine
sister sedhèrèk èstri
sit lenggah
six enem
sixteen enembelas
sixty sewidhak
size ukuran
skate sepatu es
ski ski
skin kulit
skirt rok
skull tengkorak
sky langit
sleep saré
sleeping bag kanthong kagem saré
sleeping pills pil kagem saré
slow alon
small alit
smell ambu
smile mèsem
smoke asep
smoking ngrokok
smooth (*adj.*) alus
snack (*n.*) jajanan
snake sawer
snow (*n.*) salju; (*v.*) maringi salju
soap sabun
soccer bal-balan
sock kasut
soft alus
sold kesadé; **sold out** kesadé telas
soldier prajurit
some pinten-pinten
someone priyantun

something sawijining
son laré jaler
song tembang
soon énggal
sore (*adj.*) tatu
sorry ngapunten
sound suanten
soup sop
sour asem
source sumber
south kidul
soy kedelé
spare (*adj.*) senggang; **spare part** suku cadang
speak ngendika
special khusus
speed cepet; **speed limit** wates cepet
speedometer speedometer
spell eja
spend nelasaken
spicy pedhes
spider kalamangga
spine (*n.*) lulur
spoon séndhok
sport(s) olah raga
spring rendheng
square pesagi
stadium stadion
staff staf
stairs andha
stamp perangko
stand jumeneng
standard (*n.*) standar
start miwiti
state nyatakaken
station stasiun
statue reco
stay mangg èn
steak bistik
steal colong
step jangkah
sterile steril
stitch jahitan
stolen kacolong
stomach madharan
stone séla
stop mandheg
store nyimpen
storm angin lésus
stove kompor
straight lurus
stranger tiyang manca
street margi
student siswa
study sinau
substitute penggantos
suburb padésan
subway kereta bawah tanah
sugar gendhis
suit setèlan
suitcase koper
suite dèrètan
summer ketiga
summon ngundhang
sun srengéngé
sunburn kebrangas
supermarket peken swalayan

supplies stok
surgeon dokter bedhah
surgery pambedhahan
surname asma kaluarga
surprise kagèt
surrender (*v.*) pasrah
suspect (*n.*) tersangka
swallow (*v.*) dipun lek
swear sepata
sweat kringet
sweet manis
swelling abuh
swim nglangi
symbol simbol
symptom gejala
synagogue sinagog
syringe jarum suntik
system sistem

T

table méja
tag labèl
take mundhut
talk wicanten
tall inggil
tampon tampon
tape ngrekam
taste ngraosaken
tax pajek
taxi taksi
tea tèh
teacher dwija
telephone telepon
television televisi
tell ngendhika
temperature suhu
temple candhi
temporary sawatawis
ten sedasa
tenant ingkang nyèwa
tent téndha
territory wilayah
terrorist teroris
test tès
thank you matur nuwun
that punika
theater pagelaran
then saklajengipun
there wonten ngriki
they dhèwèké
thief maling
thigh pupu
thin tipis
thing barang
think penggalih
thirsty ngelak
thirty tigang dasa
this punika
thought mikir
thousand sewu
threat inciman
three tiga
throat tenggorokan
through lumantar
throw sawat
thumb jempol
thunder bledhèk
Thursday Kemis
ticket tikèt
tie dasi

time wekdhal
tip pucuk
tire ban
today dinten punika
together sareng
toilet pakiwan; **toilet paper** tisu pakiwan
toll (*n.*) pajek
tomato tomat
tomorrow mbénjing
tonight dalu punika
tool piranti
tooth waja
toothache gerah waja
toothbrush sikat waja
toothpaste odol
top inggil
torture nyiksa
total sedayanipun
touch nyenggol
tourist turis
towel andhuk
town kutha
trade dagangan
tradition tradisi
traditional tradisional
traffic lalu lintas
trail tapak
train sepur; **train station** stasiun sepur
transfer transfer
translate nerjemahaken
translator penerjemah
transplant transplantasi
transport ngangkut
transportation transportasi
trap (*v.*) njebak
trash larahan
travel tindakan
tray nampan
treat ngrawat
trespassing nerjang
trial sidang
triangle segitiga
tribe suku
trick (*n.*) apus
trip plesir
trolley troli
trouble masalah
truck trek
trunk koper
trust percados
truth keleresan
try nyobi
true leres
Tuesday Selasa
tunnel trowongan
tutor dwija
twelve kalih welas
twenty kalih dasa
twice (*adv.*) kaping kalih

U

uncle pak lik
uncomfortable mboten sekéca
unconscious mboten sadar

underground (*adj./adv.*) wonten ngandhapipun siti
understand mangertos
underwear daleman
undo nundha
unfamiliar mboten tepang
unhappy mboten remen
uniform sragam
union perserikatan
United States Amérika Serikat
university universitas
unlock mbikak kunci
until (*conj.*) dumugi
unusual mboten kulina
up (*adv.*) minggah
use (*v.*) ndamel
usual (*adj.*) biasa

V

vacancy lowongan
vacation preinan
vaccinate vaksinasi
vanilla vanila
vegetable sayuran
vegetarian vegetarian
vehicle kendharaan
veil (*n.*) kerudung
vein nutupi
verb tembung kriya
very (*adj.*) sanget
video vidio
view pemanggih
village padésan
violence kekerasan
virus virus
visa visa
visit nuwèni
visitor dhayoh
voice swanten
volunteer relawan
vomit muntah
vote milih swanten

W

wait ngentosi
wake wungu
walk mlampah
wall témbok
wallet dompèt
want pingin
war peperangan
warm anget
warn mèngeti
warning pèngetan
wash kumbah
washing machine mesin cuci
watch ningali
water toya
we (*pron.*) kita
wear (*v.*) ngagem
weather cuaca
wedding pawiwahan
Wednesday Rebo
week minggu

weekday dinten makaryo
weekend pungkasaning minggu
weigh bobot
welcome nyambut
well (*interj.*) sakmestinipun
west kilen
what punapa
wheat gandhum
wheel rodha
wheelchair kursi rodha
when mbenjang punapa
where wonten pundi
whistle (*v.*) singsot
white pethak
who (*pron.*) sinten
why (*adv.*) kados pundi
wife garwa èstri
wild galak
win menang
wind maruta
window cendhéla
wine anggur
wing suwiwi
winter rendheng
wipe usap
wire kabel
wireless Internet internet nirkabel
wisdom kawicaksanaan
withdraw narik
withdrawal narikaken
without tanpa
woman wanita
wood kajeng
wool wol
word tembung
work nyambut damel
world donya
worm cacing
worry (*v.*) was-was
wrap (*v.*) mbungkus
wrist ugel-ugel
write nyerat
wrong lepat

X

x-ray sinar x

Y

year warsa
yeast ragi
yell nbengok
yellow jené
yes inggih
yesterday kala wingi
yogurt yogurt
you panjenengan
young (*adj.*) mudha

Z

zero nol
zipper lèrèkan
zoo kebun binatang

PHRASEBOOK

BASIC WORDS & PHRASES

Essentials

Hello.
Halo.

Goodbye.
Pareng.

Yes.
Inggih.

No.
Boten.

Excuse me. *(to get attention)*
Nuwun pirsa.

Excuse me. *(to pass)*
Nuwun sèwu.

Please.
Mangga.

Okay.
Inggih sampun.

Thank you.
Matur nuwun.

You're welcome.
Sami-sami.

Sorry.
Ngapunten.

It doesn't matter.
Boten punapa.

I need …
Kula mbetahaken …

Help!
Tulung!

Where is the bathroom?
Wonten pundi pakiwanipun?

Who?
Sinten?

What?
Punapa?

Where?
Wonten pundi

When?
Kapan?

Why?
Kénging punapa?

entrance
pintu mlebet

exit
medal

open
buka

closed
tutup

good
saé

bad
èlèk

this
puniki

that
punika

here
wonten ngriki

there
wonten ngrika

Greetings

Good morning.
Sugeng énjing.

Good afternoon.
Sugeng siyang.

Good evening.
Sugeng sonten.

Good night.
Sugeng dalu.

Welcome!
Sugeng rawuh!

How are you?
Kados pundi kahananipun?

I'm fine, thank you.
Saé-saé kemawon, matur nuwun.

And you?
Panjenenganipun?

See you …
Sugeng pepanggihan malih …

soon
énggal-énggal

later
samangké

tomorrow
mbénjang

Take care!
Ngatos-atos!

LANGUAGE DIFFICULTIES

Do you speak English?
Punapa panjenengan ngendikan ngagem basa Inggris?

Does anyone here speak English?
Punapa wonten ingkang ngendikan basa Inggris wonten ngriki?

I don't speak Javanese.
Kula mboten matur Basa Jawa.

I speak only a little Javanese.
Kula namung sekedhik matur kaliyan Basa Jawa.

I speak only English.
Kula namung matur kaliyan Basa Inggris.

Do you understand?
Punapa panjenengan pirsa?

I understand.
Kula mangertos.

I don't understand.
Kulą mboten mangertos.

What does … mean?
Punapa artosipun …?

How do you say … in Javanese language?
Kados pundi panjenengan ngendikan … ing Basa Jawa

How do you spell …?
Kados pundi panjenengan ngéja …?

Could you please …?
Punapa panjenengan saged …?

repeat that
ngambali malih

speak more slowly
ngendikan langkung alon

speak louder
ngendikana langkung sora

point out the word for me
tedahaken tembung punika dateng kula

write that down
panjenengan serataken

wait while I look it up
sawetawis kula madosi monggo dipun tengga

TRAVEL & TRANSPORTATION

Arrival, Departure, and Clearing Customs

I'm here …
Kula wonten ngriki …

> **on vacation**
> nembé preinan
>
> **for business**
> kanggé bisnis
>
> **to visit relatives**
> tindak dhateng sedhèrèk
>
> **to study**
> sinau

I'm just passing through.
Kula namung ndèrèk langkung kemawon.

I'm going to …
Kula badhé kèsah wonten …

I'm staying at …
Kula manggèn wonten …

I'm staying for X …
Kula nyepeng sadangunipun X …

days	**weeks**	**months**
dinten	minggu	wulan

You Might Hear

Punapa panjeèneèngan kagungan prekawis kanggé dipun adharaken?
Do you have anything to declare?

Punapa panjenengan ngepak piyambak?
Did you pack this on your own?

Nyuwun tulung mbikak tas punika.
Please open this bag.

Panjenengan kedah mbayar pajak kanggé punika.
You must pay duty on this.

Panjenengan nyipeng dumugi kapan?
How long are you staying?

Wonten pundi panjenengan nyipeng?
Where are you staying?

I have nothing to declare.
Kula mboten nggadah bab ingkang kedah dipun adharaken.

I'd like to declare …
Kula badhé ngadharaken …

Do I have to declare this?
Punapa kula kedah ngadharaken?

That is mine.
Punika gadhahanipun kula.

That is not mine.
Punika sanès gadhahanipun kula.

This is for personal use.
Punika kanggè pribadhi.

This is a gift.
Punika hadiyah.

I'm with a group.
Kula kaliyan rombongan.

I'm on my own.
Kula piyambakan

Here is my …
Punika … kula

boarding pass
tikèt minggah kendaraan

ticket
tikèt

ID
KTP

passport
paspor

visa
visa

You Might See

Imigrasi
Immigration

Bebas Pajek
Duty-Free

Béa Cukai
Customs

Klaim Bagasi
Baggage Claim

Kontrol Paspor
Passport control

Check-in
Check-in

Karantina
Quarantine

Polisi
Police

Warga Negara Indonesia
Indonesian citizens

Priksa keamanan
Security Check

Tiyang manca
Foreigners

Buying Tickets

Where can I buy a … ticket?
Wonten pundi kula saged tumbas tikèt …?

bus
bis

plane
pesawat

train
sepur

subway
sepur bawah tanah

one-way
bidhal kemawon

round-trip
bidhal wangsul

first class
kelas setunggal

economy class
kelas ekonomi

business class
kelas bisnis

A ticket to … please.
Nuwun sèwu, setunggal tikèt kagem …

One/Two ticket(s), please.
Nuwun sèwu, setunggal/kalih tikèt.

How much?
Reginipun pinten?

Is there a discount for …?
Punapa wanten diskon kanggé …?

children
laré alit

senior citizens
tiyang sepuh

students
siswa

tourists
turis

I have an e-ticket.
Kula gadhah tiket èlèktronik.

Can I buy a ticket on the …?
Punapa kula saged tumbas tikèt wonten …?

bus
bis

train
sepur

boat
prahu

You Might See

Lokèt tikèt
Ticket window

Panyuwunan
Reservations

Do I need to stamp the ticket?
Punapa kula kedah ngecap tikètipun?

I'd like to … my reservation.
Kula badhé … panyuwunan kula.

change
nggantos

cancel
mbatalaken

confirm
dipun konfirmasi

How long is this ticket valid for?
Tikèt punika valid dumugi kapan?

I'd like to leave …
Kula badhé késah …

I'd like to arrive …
Kula badhé dumugi …

today
dinten punika

tomorrow
mbènjang

next week
minggu ngajeng

in the morning
énjing punika

in the afternoon
siyang

in the evening
sonten

late at night
dalu

Traveling by Airplane

When is the next flight to …?
Wekdal punapa penerbangan sak lajengipun dhateng …?

Is there a bus/train to the airport?
Punapa wonten bis/sepur dhateng bandara?

How much is a taxi to the airport?
Pinten reginipun taksi dhateng bandara?

Airport, please.
Nyuwun tulung dhateng bandara.

My airline is …
Maskapai penerbangan kula …

My flight leaves at …
Penerbangan kula mangkat tabuh …

My flight number is …
Nomer penerbangan kula …

What terminal/gate?
Terminal/Gerbang ingkang pundi?

Where is the check-in desk?
Check-in wonten meja ingkang pundi?

My name is …
Nami kula …

I'm going to …
Kula badhé késah wọnten …

You Might Hear

Salajengipun!
Next!

Nuwun sewu, paspor/boarding pass panjenengan.
Your passport/boarding pass, please.

Isi kantong panjenengan monggo diwedalaken sedanten.
Empty your pockets.

Sepatu panjenengan monggo dilepas.
Take off your shoes.

Sedaya barang logam monggo dipun sèlèh ing nampan.
Place all metal items in the tray.

Penerbangan nomer …
Flight number …

Sapunika sampun minggah …
Now boarding …

Gapura nomer …
Gate number …

Is there a connecting flight?
Punapa wonten penerbangan transit?

I'd like … flight.
Kula pengin penerbangan …

a direct
langsung

a connecting
transit

an overnight
sedalu

How long is the layover?
Sepinten dangunipun transit?

I have …
Kula gadah …

one suitcase
setunggal koper

two suitcases
kalih koper

one carry-on item
setunggal tas cangking

two carry-on items
kalih tas cangking

Do I have to check this bag?
Punapa kula kedah mriksa tas puniki?

How much luggage is allowed?
Sepinten kathahipun barang ingkang pareng dibeta?

I'd like … seat.
Kulapengin kursi …

a window
caket jendéla

an aisle
caket gang

an exit row
caket pintu medal

You Might See

Check-in Check-in	**Check in tikèt èlèktronik** E-ticket check-in	
Boarding pass Boarding pass	**Minggah kendaraan** Boarding	
Keamanan Security	**Klaim bagasi** Baggage claim	
Internasional International	**Domèstik** Domestic	
Karawuhan Arrivals	**Tindak** Departures	**Transit** Connections

Can you seat us together?
Punapa panjenengan kersa lenggah sesarengan kaliyan kita?

Is the flight ...?
Punapa penerbanganipun ...?

on time	**delayed**	**cancelled**
pas wekdal	dipun undur	dipun batalaken

Where is the baggage claim?
Wonten pundi panggènan nuntut barang gawan?

I've lost my luggage.
Kula kècalan bagasi

My luggage has been stolen.
Bagasi kula dicolong

My suitcase is damaged.
Koper kula rusak

Traveling by Train

Which line goes to … station?
Pundi jalur ingkang dumugi stasiun …?

Is it direct?
Punapa menika jalur langsung?

Is it an express/local train?
Punapa punika sepur ekspres?

I'd like to take the bullet/high-speed train.
Kula badhé nitih sepur cepat.

Do I have to change trains?
Punapa kula kedah gantos sepur?

Can I have a schedule?
Punapa saged kula nyuwun jadual?

When is the last train back?
Wekdal punapa sepur ingkang pungkasan wangsul malih?

Which track?
Jalur ingkang pundhi?

Where is track …?
Wonten pundi jalur …?

Where is/are the ...?
Wonten pundi ...?

dining car
gerbong dhahar

information desk
meja informasi

luggage lockers
loker kanggé koper

reservations desk
meja reservasi/pesenan

ticket machine
mesin tikèt

ticket office
kantor tikèt

waiting room
ruang tengga

This is my seat.
Punika kursi kulaa.

Here is my ticket.
Punika tikèt kula.

Can I change seats?
Punapa kula saged pindhah kursi?

What station is this?
Punika stasiun punapa?

What is the next station?
Salajengipun stasiun punapa?

Does this train stop at …?
Punapa sepur punika mandhap dateng …?

Traveling by Bus and Subway

Which bus do I take for …?
Pundi bis ingkang kula pundhut kanggé dhateng …?

Which subway do I take for …?
Pundi sepur bawah tanah ingkang kula pundhut dhateng …?

Which …?
Pundi …?

gate	**line**	**stop**	**station**
gerbang	jalur	mandeg	stasiun

Where is the nearest bus stop?
Wonten pundi halte bis ingkang paling celak?

Where is the nearest subway station?
Wonten pundi stasiun sepur bawah tanah ingkang paling celak?

Can I have a bus map?
Punapa saged kula nyuwun peta bis?

Can I have a subway map?
Punapa saged kula nyuwun peta sepur bawah tanah?

How far is it?
Sepinten tebihipun?

How do I get to …?
Kados pundhi kula dumugi wonten …?

Is this the bus to …?
Punapa bis punika dumugi wonten …?

Is this the subway to …?
Punapa sepur bawah tanah punika dhateng …?

When is the … bus to …?
Kapan bis ingkang dhateng … …?

first	**next**	**last**
sepindhah	salajengipun	pungkasan

Do I have to change buses/trains?
Punapa kula kedah gantos bis/kereta?

Where do I transfer?
Wonten pundi kula transit?

Can you tell me when to get off?
Punapa saged panjenengan sanjang kula kapan badhé mandap?

How many stops to …?
Kaping pinten mandeg kanggé dhateng …?

Where are we?
Kita wonten pundi?

Next stop, please!
Nuwun sewu, mandeg salajengipun!

You Might See

halte bis
bus stop

stasiun sepur bawah tanah
subway station

lawang mlebet
entrance

medal
exit

Stop here, please!
Nuwun sewu, mandeg dhateng mriki

Traveling by Taxi

Taxi!
Taksi!

Where can I get a taxi?
Wontèn pundi kula saged pikantuk taksi?

Can you call a taxi?
Punapa saged panjenengan nimbali taksi?

I'd like a taxi now.
Kula pengin taksi sapunika.

I'd like a taxi in an hour.
Kula pengin taksi setunggal jam malih.

Pick me up at ...
Susul kula wontèn ...

Take me to …
Beta kula dhateng …

this address
alamat punika

the airport
bandara

the train station
stasiun sepur

the bus station
terminal bis

Can you take a different route?
Punapa saged panjenengan mendhet rute ingkang sanès?

Can you drive faster/slower?
Punapa saged panjenengan nyupir langkung cepet/alon?

Stop/Wait here.
Mandeg/Tengga dhateng ngriki.

How much will it cost?
Reginipun dados pinten?

You said it would cost …
Panjènengan ngendikan reginipun …

Keep the change.
Monggo disimpen lintunipun.

Traveling by Car

Renting a Car

Where is the car rental?
Wonten pundi panggènan sewa mobil?

I'd like …
Kula badhé …

a cheap car
mobil ingkang mirah

a compact car
mobil ingkang ringkas

a van
van

an SUV
SUV

an automatic transmission
transmisi otomatis

a manual transmission
transmisi manual

a scooter
sekuter

a motorcycle
sepeda motor

air conditioning
pendhingin udara

a child seat
kursi laré alit

How much does it cost …?
Reginipun … pinten?

per day
saben dintèn

per week
saben minggu

per kilometer
saben kilometer

for unlimited mileage
kangge jarak tempuh ingkang mboten winates

with full insurance
kaliyan asuransi penuh

What kind of fuel does it use?
Bahan bakaripun punapa?

Are there any discounts?
Punapa wonten potongan?

I (don't) have an international driver's license.
Kula (mboten) gadhah SIM internasional.

I don't need it until …
Kula dereng mbetahaken ngantos …

Monday
Senin

Tuesday
Selasa

Wednesday
Rebo

Thursday
Kemis

Friday
Jumuah

Saturday
Setu

Sunday
Ahad

You Might Hear

Kula betah simpenan.
I'll need a deposit.

Nami inisial wonten mriki.
Inital here.

Tapak asma wonten mriki.
Sign here.

Fuel and Repairs

Where's the gas station?
Pom bensin wonten pundi?

Fill it up.
Dipun isi ngantos kebak.

I need …
Kula betah …

gas
bènsin

diesel
solar

leaded
bertimbal

unleaded
tanpa timbal

regular
biasa

super
super

premium
premium

You Might See

swalayan
self-service

layanan penuh
full-service

Check the …
Priksa …

battery
aki

brakes
rem

headlights
lampu ngajeng

oil
oli

radiator
radiator

taillights
lampu rem

tires
ban

transmission
kopling

The car broke down.
Mobilipun mogok.

The car won't start.
Mobilipun mboten saged urip.

I ran out of gas.
Kula ketelasen bènsin

I have a flat tire.
Ban kula kempés

I need a ...
Kula betah ...

jumper cable
kabel jumper

mechanic
montir

tow truck
truk dèrèk

Can you fix the car?
Punapa panjenengan saged ndandosimobil?

When will it be ready?
Kapan mobilipun siaga?

Driving Around

Can I park here?
Punapa saged kula parkir wonten mriki?

Where's the parking lot/garage?
Wontèn pundi panggenan kanggé parkir/garasi?

How much does it cost?
Reginipun pinten?

Is parking free?
Punapa parkiripun mboten bayar?

What's the speed limit?
Watès kecepatanipun pinten?

How much is the toll?
Bea tolipun pinten?

You Might See

Mandeg
Stop

Dipun sumanggaaken
Yield

Setunggal arah
One-way

Boten pareng mlebet
Do not enter

Batas kecepatan
Speed limit

Can I turn here?
Punapa saged kula menggok wonten mriki?

Problems with a Car

There's been an accident.
Wonten kacilakan.

Call the police/ambulance.
Nimbali polisi/ambulan.

My car has been stolen.
Mobil kula dicolong.

My license plate number is …
Nomer plat kendaraan kula …

Can I have your insurance information?
Punapa panjenengan saged maringi informasi ngengingi asuransi?

Getting Directions

Excuse me, please!
Numun sewu!

Can you help me?
Punapa panjenengan saged mbiyantu kula?

Is this the way to …?
Punapa punika margi dhateng …?

How far is it to …?
Sepinten tebihipun dhateng …?

Is this the right road to …?
Punapa punika margi ingkang leres dhateng …?

How much longer until we get to …?
Sepinten dangunipun kita nembé dumugi …?

Where's …?
Wontèn pundi …?

… Street
Margi …

this address
alamat puniki

the highway
margi ageng

the downtown area
pusat kutha

Where am I?
Kula wonten pundi?

You Might Hear

Nitih …
Take …

wod
the bridge

medal
the exit

terowongan
the tunnel

margi ageng
the highway

bunderan
the traffic circle

Margi/MargiAgeng …
… Street/Avenue

Can you show me on the map?
Punapa panjenengan saged nedhahaken panggènan kula wonten péta?

Do you have a road map?
Punapa panjenengan kagungan péta?

How do I get to …?
Kadospundi kula dumugi ing …?

How long does it take …?
Sepinten dangunipun nganggé …?

on foot
mlampah

by car
nitih mobil

using public transportation
ngagem transportasi umum

I'm lost.
Kula kesasar.

You Might Hear

Mlampah lurus kemawon.
Go straight ahead.

Mènggok nengen.
Turn right.

Mènggok kiwa
Turn left.

seberang margi
across the street

sekitar pojokan
around the corner

maju
forward

mundur
backward

wonten ngajengipun
in front (of)

wingking
behind

ing persimpangan salajengipun
at the next intersection

ing lampu setopan salajengipun
at the next traffic light

caket kaliyan
next to

caket
near

tebih
far

sadèrèngipun
before

sasampunipun
after

lor
north

kidul
south

wètan
east

kulon
west

ACCOMMODATIONS

Can you recommend …?
Punapa panjenengan saged nyaranaken …?

a hotel hotèl	**a motel** motél
an inn panginepan	**a bed-and-breakfast** nginep pikantuk sarapan
a guesthouse panginepan	**a (youth) hostel** hostél

Where is the nearest …?
Pundi … ingkang langkung caket?

I'm looking for … accommodations.
Kula pados akomodasi ingkang …

inexpensive mirah	**luxurious** méwah
traditional tradisional	**clean** resik
conveniently located lokasinipun nyaman	

Is there English-speaking staff?
Punapa wonten staf ingkang ngendikan ndamel basa Inggris?

Staying At a Hotel

Booking a Room and Checking in

vacancy	**no vacancy**
kamar kosong	mboten wonten kamar kosong

Do you have any rooms available?
Punapa wonten kamar kosong?

I'd like a room for tonight.
Kula pesen setunggal kamar kanggé dalu punika.

Can I make a reservation?
Punapa saged kula pesen kamar?

I'd like to reserve a room …
Kula pengin pesen kamar …

for XX nights
kagem xx dalu

for one person
kagem setunggal tiyang

for two people
kagem tiyang kalih

with a queen-size bed
kasur ukuran nomer kalih

with two beds
kaliyan kalih kasur

How much is it?
Reginipun pinten?

How much is it per night/person?
Reginipun setunggal dalu/tiyang pinten?

Does that include sales tax (VAT)?
Punapa sampun kalebet pajak?

Can I pay by credit card?
Punapa saged kula mbayar ndamel kertu krédit?

Is breakfast included?
Punapa kalebet sarapan?

My credit card number is …
Nomer kertu kredit kula …

Do you have …?
Punapa panjenengan kagungan …?

air conditioning pendingin udara
a business center pusat bisnis
cots pondok
a crib ambèn bayi
an elevator lift
a gym panggenan olahraga
hot water toya bentèr
a kitchen pawon
laundry service layanan binatu
linens linen
a microwave microwave
non-smoking rooms kamar bebas rokok
phones télépon
a pool kolam
private bathrooms padusan pribadhi
a restaurant restoran

room service layanan kamar
a safe kotak pengaman
television tivi
towels anduk
wireless Internet internet nirkabel

Is there a curfew?
Punapa wonten jam malam?

When is check-in?
Kapan wekdalipun daftar?

May I see the room?
Punapa kula pareng ningali kamaripun?

How can somebody call my room?
Kados pundi tiyang saged nelpon kamar kula?

Do you have anything …?
Punapa panjenengan kagungan ingkang …?

bigger
langkung ageng

cleaner
langkung resik

quieter
langkung sepi

less expensive
langkung mirah

I'll take it.
Kula pundhut.

I don't have a reservation.
Kula boten nggadahi pesenan.

I have a reservation under …
Kula pesen ndamel asma …

Is the room ready?
Punapa kamaripun sampun sumadya?

When will the room be ready?
Kapan kamaripun sumadya?

room number	**floor**	**room key**
kamar nomer	jogan	kunci kamar

At the Hotel

Where is the ...?
Wonten pundi ...?

bar bar
bathroom pakiwan
convenience store toko serba ada
dining room ruang dhahar
drugstore apoték
elevator lift
information desk meja informasi
lobby lobi
pool kolam renang
restaurant restoran
shower pancuran

Can I have ...?
Punapa saged kula nyuwun ...?

a blanket selimut
another room key kunci kamar sanès
a pillow bantal
a plug for the bath sumpel bak mandi

soap sabun
clean sheets seprèi resik
towels anduk
toilet paper tisu pakiwan
a wake-up call at … telepon nggigah jam …

I would like to place these items in the safe.
Kula badhe nyimpen barang punika dhateng kotak pengaman.

I would like to retrieve my items from the safe.
Kula badhe mendet barang kula saking kotak pengaman.

Can I stay an extra night?
Punapa saged kula nambah nyipeng?

Problems at a Hotel

There's a problem with the room.
Wonten prekawis dhateng kamar punika.

The … doesn't work.
… nipun mboten fungsi.

air conditioning Pendhingin udara
door lock Kunci lawang
hot water Toya bentèr
shower Pancuran
sink Kran
toilet Pakiwan/wc

The lights won't turn on.
Lampunipun pejah.

The ... aren't clean.
... mboten resik.

pillows	**sheets**	**towels**
Bantal	Selimut	Anduk

The room has bugs/mice.
Kamaripun wonten serangga/tikus.

The room is too noisy.
Kamaripun ramé sanget.

I've lost my key.
Kula kecalan kunci.

I've locked myself out.
Kula kekunci saking njawi.

Checking Out

When is check-out?
Kapan check out ipun?

When is the earliest/latest I can check out?
Kapan kula saged check out paling rumiyin/terakhir?

I would like to check out.
Kula pingin check out.

I would like a receipt.
Kula nyuwun kwitansi.

I would like an itemized bill.
Kula nyuwun rincian nota.

There's a mistake on this bill.
Wonten kesalahan ing nota puniki.

Please take this off the bill.
Nuwun sewu nota puniki dipun bucal.

The total is incorrect.
Jumlah totalipun salah

I would like to pay …
Kula badhe mbayar …

by credit card
kaliyan kertu kredit

in cash
kontan

by (traveler's) check
kaliyan cek (wisatawan)

Can I leave my bags here until …?
Punapa kula saged tilaraken tas kula ing mriki dumugi …?

Renting Other Accommodations

I'd like to rent …
Kula kepingin nyewa …

an apartment	**a room**	**a house**
apartemén	kamar	griya

How much is it per week?
Reginipun per minggu pinten?

I intend to stay for XX months.
Kula pengin manggèn xx wulan.

Is it furnished?
Punapa wonten perabotipun?

Does it have …?
Punapa niki kagungan …?

a kitchen pawon
dishes piranti dhahar
cooking utensils piranti masak
a washing machine mesin cuci
a room kamar
a dryer pengering rasukan
linens linen
towels anduk

Do you require a deposit?
Punapa panjenengan mbetahaken simpenan?

When is the rent due?
Kapan batas séwanipun telas?

Who is the superintendent?
Sinten pengawasipun?

Who should I contact for repairs?
Sinten ingkang kedah kula hubungi kanggé?

Camping and the Outdoors

campsite
lokasi kèmah

Can I camp here?
Punapa kula saged kèmah wonten mriki?

Where should I park?
Kula parkir wonten pundi?

Do you have … for rent?
Punapa panjenengan kagungan … kanggé dipun sèwa?

tents tènda
sleeping bags kantong tidur
cooking equipment piranti masak

Do you have …
Punapa panjenengan kagungan …

a shower block pancuran
electricity listrik
laundry facilities fasilitas binatu

How much is it per …?
Pinten reginipun per …?

lot	**person**	**night**
lokasi	tiyang	dalu

Are there … that I should be careful of?
Punapa wonten … ingkang kedah kula waspadai?

animals	**plants**	**insects**
kewan	tetanduran	hama

DINING OUT

Meals

breakfast	dhahar ènjang
lunch	dhahar siyang
brunch	dhahar ènjang kaliyan siyang
dinner	dhahar dalu
a snack	jajanan
dessert	dhaharan panutup

Finding a Place to Eat

Can you recommend …?
Punapa panjenengan saged nyaranaken …?

a good restaurant
restoran ingkang saé

a restaurant with local dishes
restoran ingkang nyawisaken dhaharan lokal

an inexpensive restaurant
restoran ingkang mirah

a popular bar
bar ingkang kondang

I'm hungry.
Kula luwé.

I'm thirsty.
Kula ngelak.

Types of Restaurants

bar
bar

bistro
bistro

buffet
prasmanan

café
kafé

fast food restaurant
restoran cepet saji

halal restaurant
restoran halal

kosher restaurant
restoran kosher

pizzeria
warung pizza

restaurant
restoran

snack bar
warung jajan

steakhouse
griya bistik

teahouse
griya teh

vegetarian restaurant
restoran vegetarian

vegan restaurant
restoran vegan

Reservations and Getting a Table

I have a reservation for …
Kula pesen kagem …

The reservation is under …
Pesenan kagem …

I'd like to reserve a table for …
Kula pengin pesen meja-kagem …

Can we sit ...?
Punapa saged kula lenggah ...?

over here
wonten ngriki

over there
wọnten ngrika

by a window
caket jendhéla

outside
wonten njawi

in a non-smoking area
wonten daerah bebas rokok

How long is the wait?
Nengganipun sepinten dangu?

It's for here.
Punika kagem ngriki.

It's to go.
Punika ajeng tindak.

Ordering

Waiter! / Waitress!
Rencang!

Excuse me!
Nuwun sèwu!

I'd like to order.
Kula badhé ndèrèk pesen.

Can I have ... please?
Punapa kula saged pikantuk ...?

a menu
menu

a children's menu
menu kangge laré alit

a wine list
dhaptar anggur

a drink menu
menu unjukan

Do you have a menu in English?
Punapa wonten menu ing basa Inggris?

Do you have a set/fixed price menu?
Punapa panjenengan kagungan menu ingkang reginipun tetep?

What are the specials?
Punapa pasugatan ingkang istimewa?

Do you have …?
Punapa panjenengan kagungan …?

Can you recommend some local dishes?
Punapa panjenengan saged maringi pirsa pasugatan lokal?

What do you recommend?
Punapa ingkang panjenengan saranaken?

I'll have …
Kula badhé nedha …

What's this?
Punika punapa?

What's in this?
Isinipun punapa?

Is it …?
Punapa niki …?

spicy
pedhes

bitter
pait

sweet
legi

hot
bnter

cold
asrep

Do you have any vegetarian dishes?
Punapa panjenengan kagungan pasugatan vegetarian?

I'd like it with …
Kula kepingin punika kaliyan …

I'd like it without …
Kula kepingin punika tanpa …

Are there any drink specials?
Punapa wonten unjukan ingkang paling istiméwa?

Can I see the drink menu/wine list?
Punapa kula saged mirsani menu unjukan/ dhaptar anggur?

Can I have …?
Punapa saged kula pikantuk …?

a glass of …
setunggal gelas …

a bottle of…
setunggal botol …

a pitcher of …
setunggal teko …

I'd like a bottle of …
Kula pengin setunggal botol …

red wine
anggur abrit

white wine
anggur pethak

rosé wine
anggur mawar

the house wine
anggur griya

dessert wine
anggur pencuci mulut

champagne
sampanye

dry wine
anggur garing

A light/dark beer, please.
Nyuwun tulung bir biasa/pekat.

Special Dietary Needs

Is this dish free of animal product?
Punapa dhaharan punika bébas saking produk hewani?

I'm allergic to …
Kula alergi …

I can't eat …
Kula mbọten saged nedha …

dairy produk susu
egg tigan
gelatin gelatin
gluten ketan
meat daging
MSG Micin
nuts kacang polong
peanuts kacang brol
seafood dhaharan laut
spicy foods dhaharan pedhes
wheat gandum

I'm diabetic.
Kula gadhah penyakit diabètes.

Do you have any sugar-free products?
Punapa panjenengan kagungan produk bebas gula?

Do you have any artificial sweeteners?
Punapa panjenengan kagungan pemanis buatan?

I'm vegan/vegetarian.
Kula vegetarian.

I'm on a special diet.
Kula nembé diet khusus.

Complaints at a Restaurant

This isn't what I ordered.
Punika sanès pesenan kula.

I ordered …
Kula pesen …

This is …
Niki …

cold asrep
spoiled mambet
not fresh mboten seger
too spicy pedes sanget
too tough alot sanget
not vegetarian sanès vegetarian

undercooked kirang mateng
overcooked kematengen

Can you take it back, please?
Nyuwun tulung dipun beta malih?

I cannot eat this.
Kula mboten saged nedha ingkang niki.

We're leaving.
Kula kesah.

How much longer until we get our food?
Sapinten dangunipun dhaharan punika dumugi panggènan kawula?

We cannot wait any longer.
Kula mboten saged nengga malih.

Paying at a Restaurant

Check, please!
Nuwun sewu notanipun!

We'd like to pay separately.
Kula badhé mbayar piyambak-piyambak.

Can we have separate checks?
Punapa saged kawula pikantuk nota ingkang pisah?

We're paying together.
Kula mbayar sesarengan.

Is service included?
Punapa sampun termasuk layanan?

What is this charge for?
Punika beaya kangge punapa?

There is a mistake in this bill.
Nota puniki klintu.

I didn't order that. I ordered …
Kula mboten pesen punika. Kula pesen …

Can I have a receipt, please?
Saged nyuwun kuitansinipun?

Can I have an itemized bill, please?
Saged nyuwun nota ingkang sampun dipun rinci?

It was delicious!
Dhaharanipun eco!

FOOD & DRINK

Cooking Methods

baked dipun panggang
boiled dipun godhog
braised dipun tumis kenthel
breaded dipun lapisi tepung roti
creamed dipun olesi krim
diced dipun iris dadhu
filleted dipun iris tipis
grilled dipun bakar
microwaved dipun masak ndamel mikrowave
mixed dipun campur
poached dipun godhog
re-heated dipun panasaken malih
roasted dipun panggang
sautéed dipun tumis cepet
smoked diasep
steamed dipun kukus
stewed dipun godhog
stir-fried dipun osèng
stuffed dipun isi
toasted dipun panggang

rare mentah
medium rare setengah mateng
well-done mateng

on the side sepalih

Tastes

bitter pait
sweet legi
bland anyep
sour kecut
salty asin
spicy pedhes

Dietary Terms

decaffeinated dipun wedalaken kandungan zat kafeinipun
free-range dipun umbar
genetically modified dipun ewahi nganggé cara genetis
gluten-free bebas ketan
kosher kosher
low-fat rendhah lemak
low in cholesterol rendhah kolestrol
low in sugar rendhah gula
organic organik
salt-free bebas uyah
vegan vegan
vegetarian vegetarian

Breakfast Foods

bacon daging babi asep
bread roti
butter mentèga
cereal sèrèal
cheese kèju
eggs tigan
granola granola
honey madu
jam/jelly selai
omelet tigan dadar
sausage sosis
yogurt yogurt

Vegetables

asparagus asparagus
avocado alpukat
beans kacang
broccoli brokoli
cabbage kol
carrot wortel
cauliflower kembang kol
celery godhong selèdri
chickpeas buncis
corn jagung
cucumber timun
eggplant tèrong
garlic bawang pethak
lentils lentil
lettuce godhong seladha
mushroom jamur
olives zaitun
onion brambang
peas kacang polong
pepper paprika
potato kentang
radish lobak
spinach godhong bayem
sweet potato ketela
tomato tomat

Fruits and Nuts

apricot aprikot
apple apel
banana gedhang
blueberry bluberi
cashew mété
cherry ceri
coconut kelapa
date korma
fig ara
grape anggur
grapefruit jeruk bali
lemon jeruk nipis
lime jeruk limun
mandarin mandarin
melon mèlon
orange jeruk
peanut kacang
peach persik
pear pir
pineapple nanas
plum prem
pomegranate delima
raspberry rapsberi
strawberry stroberi
tangerine jeruk keprok
walnut kenari
watermelon semangka

Meats

beef sapi
burger roti isi daging
chicken ayam
duck bèbèk
goat mendo
ham ham
lamb wedhus
pork babi
rabbit kelinci
steak bistik
turkey kalkun
veal daging sapi nom

Seafood

calamari cumi-cumi
crab yuyu
fish iwak
lobster lobster
octopus gurita
salmon salmon
shrimp urang

Desserts

cake jajan
cookie jajanan ingkang garing
ice cream es krim

Drinks

Non-alcoholic Drinks

apple juice jus apel
coffee (black) kopi (kenthel)
coffee with milk kopi susu
hot chocolate coklat panas
lemonade lèmon
milk susu

mineral water toya mineral
orange juice jus jeruk
sparkling water toya soda
soda / soft drink soda / softdrink
soymilk susu kedhelé
tea tèh

Alcoholic Drinks

... beer bir ...
- **bottled** wadhah botol
- **draft** tong
- **canned** wadhah kalèng

brandy brèndi
champagne sampanye
cocktail koktail
gin gin
liqueur arak
margarita margarita
martini martini
rum rum
scotch scotch
tequila tequila
vermouth vermouth
vodka vodka
whiskey wiski
wine anggur
- **dessert wine** anggur penutup
- **dry wine** anggur dry
- **red wine** anggur abrit
- **rosé wine** anggur jambon
- **white wine** anggur pethak

Grocery Shopping

Where is the nearest market/supermarket?
Wonten pundi peken ingkang langkung celak?

Where are the baskets/carts?
Wonten pundhi kranjang kerèta nipun?

I'd like some of this/that.
Kula pengin niki sekedhik.

Can I have ...?
Punapa kula saged angsal ...?

a (half) kilo of ... sepalih kilo ...
a liter of ... setunggal liter ...
a piece of ... setunggal iris ...
a little more sekedik malih
a little less dipun kirangi sekedik

Where can I find ...
Wonten pundi kula saged angsal ...

cleaning products produk pembersih
dairy products produk susu
the deli section makanan mateng
fresh produce bahan ingkang seger
fresh fish ulam seger
frozen foods jajaran beku
household goods perkakas griya
meats daging
poultry produk unggas

You Might See

Dipun sade kaliyan …
Sell by …

Dipun sèlèh wonten kulkas.
Keep refrigerated.

Dipuntelasaken … dinten saksampunipun dipun bikak.
Eat within … days of opening.

Dipun panasi malih sadèrèngipun dipun dhahar.
Reheat before consuming.

kosher
kosher

organik
organic

Cècèk kanggé végetarian
Suitable for vegetarians

saged dipun masak ndamel mikrowave
microwaveable

I need to go to …
kula pengin tindak dateng …

the bakery tukang roti
the butcher shop toko daging
the convenience store toko serba ada
the fish market peken ulam
the produce market pasar indhuk
the supermarket swalayan

gram(s) gram

kilo(s) kilo

a piece of …
setunggal potong …

two pieces of …
kalih potong …

Can I have a little/lot of … please?
Punapa kula saged angsal … sekedhik/kathah?

That's enough, thanks.
Cekap, matur nuwun.

a bottle setunggal botol
a jar setunggal toples
a packet setunggal bungkus
a box setunggal kotak

Paying for Groceries

Where is the checkout?
Kasiripun wonten pundi?

Do I pay here?
Punapa leres kula mbayar ing ngriki?

Do you accept credit cards?
Punapa panjenengan nampi kertu kredit

I'll pay in cash.
Kula badhé mbayar lunas.

I'll pay by credit card.
Kula badhé mbayar ngagem kertu kredit.

Paper/Plastic, please.
Nuwun sewu kertasi/plastikipun

I don't need a bag.
Kula mboten betah tas.

I have my own bag.
Kula gadhah tas piyambak

MONEY

Currency and Conversion

Where can I exchange money?
Wonten pundi kula saged lintu arta?

Is there a currency exchange office nearby?
Punapa ing caket mriki wonten kantor kangge lintu arta?

I'd like to exchange … for …
Kula bade ngijolaken … kaliyan …

U.S. dollars
dolar Amerika

pounds
ponsterling

Canadian dollars
dolar Kanada

Euros
yuro

traveler's checks
cek turis

What is the exchange rate?
Tarip lintunipun pinten?

What is the commission change?
Pinten komisinipun?

Can you write that down for me?
Punapa panjenengan saged nyerat kagem kula?

Banking

Is there a bank near here?
Punapa ing celak ngriki wonten bank?

Where is the nearest ATM?
Wonten pundi ATM ingkang celak?

What time does the bank open/close?
Jam pinten bank buka/tutup?

Can I cash this check here?
Punapa cèk punika saged kula dadosaken arta ing ngriki?

I would like to get a cash advance.
Kula pingin pikantuk arta.

I would like to cash some traveler's checks.
Kula pingin ndadosaken arta cek turis punika.

I've lost my traveler's checks.
Kula kècalan cek turis kula.

The ATM ate my card.
ATM nipun mendhet kertu kula.

You Might See at an ATM

lebetaken kertunipun
insert card

nomer PIN
PIN number

lebetaken
enter

dipun busek
clear

batalaken
cancel

priksa
checking

tabungan
savings

mendhet tabungan
withdrawal

setor
deposit

kuitansi
receipt

SHOPPING & SERVICES

Shopping

Where's the ...?
Wonten pundi ...?

antiques store toko barang antik
bakery toko roti
bookstore toko buku
camera store toko kaméra
clothing store toko busana
convenience store toserba
delicatessen toko masakan mateng
department store toserba
electronics store toko èlèktronik
gift shop toko kado
health food store toko dhaharan sèhat
jeweler tukang emas
liquor store warung minuman keras
mall mall
market peken
music store toko musik
pastry shop warung jajanan
pharmacy toko obat
shoe store toko sepatu
souvenir store toko suvenir
supermarket swalayan
toy store toko dolanan

Getting Help in a Store

Where's the...?
Wonten pundi ...?

> **cashier** kasir
> **escalator** eskalator
> **elevator** lift
> **fitting room** kamar pas
> **store map** peta toko

Can you help me?
Punapa panjenengan saged mbiyantu kula?

I'm looking for ...
Kula madosi ...

Where can I find ...?
Wonten pundi kula saged manggihaken ...?

I would like ...
Kula pingin ...

I'm just looking.
Kula namung mirsani.

Preferences

I want something ...
Kula kepingin ingkang ...

big	**small**
ageng	alit

cheap	**expensive**
mirah	awis
local	**nice**
lokal	saé

I can only pay …
Kula namung saged mbayar …

Is it authentic?
Punapa niki asli?

Can you show me that?
Punapa panjenengan saged nedahaken punika dateng kula?

Can I see it?
Punapa saged kula mirsani?

Do you have any others?
Punapa panjenengan kagungan sanesipun?

Can you ship this?
Punapa panjenengan saged ngintunaken niki?

Can you wrap this?
Punapa panjenengan saged wungkus niki?

Do you have anything lighter?
Punapa wonten werni ingkang langkung padang?

Do you have anything darker?
Punapa wonten werni ingkang langkung peteng?

Do you have this in …?
Punapa panjenengan kagungan ingkang werninipun …?

black	cemeng
blue	biru
brown	coklat
gray	abu-abu
green	ijem
orange	oranye
pink	jambon
purple	ungu
red	abrit
white	pethak
yellow	jené

Haggling

That's too expensive.
Punika kawisen.

Do you have anything cheaper?
Punapa panjenengan gadhah ingkang langkung mirah?

I'll give you …
Kula badhe mbayar panjenengan …

I'll have to think about it.
Kula pikìr rumiyin

Is that your best price?
Punapa menika regi paling pas?

Can you give me a discount?
Punapa kula saged nyuwun diskon

Deciding

That's not quite what I want.
Punika sanes ingkang kulą pingini.

I don't like it.
Kula mboten remen.

It's too expensive.
Punika awis sanget.

I'll take it.
Kula pundhut.

Paying at a Store

Where can I pay?
Wonten pundi kula saged mbayar?

How much?
Pinten?

Does the price include tax?
Punapa reginipun sampun kalebet pajek?

I'll pay in cash.
Kula badhé mbayar lunas.

I'll pay by credit card.
Kula badhé mbayar ngagem kertu kredit.

Do you accept traveler's checks?
Punapa panjenengan nampi cek turis?

I have …
Kula gadhah …

an ATM card	kertu ATM
a credit card	kertu kredit
a debit card	kertu debit
a gift card	kertu hadiyah

Can I have a receipt?
Kula saged nyuwun kuitansi

Complaining at a Store

This is broken.
Punika risak

It doesn't work.
Punika mboten saged didamel.

I'd like …
Kula pingin …

to exchange this ngijolaken niki
to return this mangsulaken niki
a refund mangsulaken arto
to speak to the manager matur kaliyan manajer

Grocery Shopping *See pages 131-134*
Pharmacy *See pages 184-187*

Services

bank bank
barber tukang cukur
dry cleaner binatu
hair salon salon rikma
laundromat londri
nail salon salon kuku
spa spa
travel agency agen perjalanan

At a Hair Salon / Barber

I'd like a …
Kula pingin …

color semir rikma
cut kethok rikma
perm permanen
shave cukur jenggot
trim ngrapikaken rikma

Cut about this much off.
Dipun kethok sewiyar niki.

Can I have a shampoo?
Punapa saged kula nyuwun shampo?

Cut it shorter here.
Kethok langkung cekak ing ngriki.

Leave it longer here.
Kersanipun wiyar ing ngriki.

At a Spa

I'd like (a) …
Kula pingin …

acupuncture akupuntur
aromatherapy aromaterapi
facial rawat pasuryan
manicure manikur
massage pijet
pedicure pedikur
sauna mandi uap
wax ngresiki ngagem lilin

At a Laundromat

Is there …?
Punapa punika …?

full-service
layanan ingkang jangkep?

self-service
swalayan

same-day service
layanan setunggal dinten dados

Do you have …?
Punapa panjenengan kagungan …?

bleach pemutih
change susuk
detergent sabun cuci

dryer sheets seprei ingkang langkung garing
fabric softener pelembut kain

This machine is broken.
Mesin punika risak.

How does this work?
Kados pundi cara ngginaaken?

When will my clothes be ready?
Kapan rasukan kula siap?

whites rasukan pethak
colors rasukan warna
delicates rasukan ingkang seratipun alus

hand wash dipun umbah asta
gentle cycle puteran alus
permanent press dipun près
dry clean only dipun kumbah garing mawon

cold water toya asrep
warm water toya anget
hot water toya bentèr

At a Bank *See page 136*

SOCIAL INTERACTION

Introductions

Hello. Halo. **Hi!** Hai!

Sir Bapak **Madam** Ibu

Mr. Tn. **Ms.** Nn. **Mrs.** Ny.

Dr. *(medical)* Dr. *(kesehatan)*
Dr. *(academic)* Dr. *(akademik)*

What's your name?
Asma panjenengan sinten?

> **My name is …**
> Nami kula …

Pleased to meet you.
Remen kepanggih panjenengan.

What do you do?
Punapa pendamelan panjenengan?

> **I'm a student.**
> Kula siswa.

> **I work for …**
> Kula nyambut damel wonten …

> **I'm retired.**
> Kula sampun pensiun.

How old are you?
Yuswanipun panjenengan pinten?

I am … years old.
Kula … warsa.

Etiquette

How are you?
Punapa pawartosipun?

Fine, thanks.
Saé, matur nuwun.

And you?
Panjenengan?

Good morning.	Sugeng enjing.
Good afternoon.	Sugeng siang.
Good evening.	Sugeng sonten.
Good night.	Sugeng dalu.

See you …
Sugeng pepanggihan malih …

later	mangké
soon	énggal- énggal
tomorrow	mbénjing

Welcome! Sugeng rawuh!
Goodbye. Pareng, nyuwun pamit.

Please. Sumangga.

Thank you. Matur nuwun.

You're welcome. Sami-sami.

I'm sorry. Pangapunten.

Excuse me. Nuwun sèwu.

Interests & Leisure

Do you like ...?
Punapa panjenengan remen ...?

art seni
cinema bioskop
music musik
sports olah raga
theater teater

Yes, very much.
Inggih, remen sanget.

Not really.
Mboten patos remen.

A little.
Sekedik.

I like ...
Kula remen ...

I don't like ...
Kula mboten remen ...

Can you recommend a good …?
Punapa panjenengan saged nyaranaken … ingkang saé?

book buku
CD CD
exhibit pameran
museum musium
film film
play drama

What's playing tonight?
Punapa ingkang dipun puter dalupunika?

I like … (films)
Kula remen (pilm) …

action èksen
art seni
comedy dagelan
drama drama
foreign asing
horror medèni
indie indie
musical musikal
mystery misteri
romance asmara
suspense tegang

What are the movie times?
Tabuh pinten pilm dipun wiwiti?

Sports

I like ...
Kula remen …

baseball besbol
basketball basket
bicycling sepedahan
boxing tinju
diving nyelam
golf golf
hiking minggah gunung
martial arts bela diri
skiing main ski
soccer bal-balan
surfing selancar
swimming renang
tennis tènes
volleyball voli

When's the game?
Mbénjang punapa pertandinganipun?

Would you like to go to the game with me?
Punapa panjenengan kersa tindak wonten pertandingan kaliyan kula?

What's the score?
Pinten bijinipun?

Who's winning?
Sinten ingkang menang?

Do you want to play?
Punapa panjenengan kersa dolanan?

Can I join in?
Punapa pareng kula nggabung?

Friends and Romance

What are your plans for ...?
Punapa rencana panjenengan kagem ...?

tonight dalu punika
tomorrow mbénjing
the weekend akhir pekan

Would you like to get a drink?
Punapa panjenengan kersa ngunjuk?

Where would you like to go?
Panjenengan pingin tindak dathengpundi?

Would you like to go dancing?
Punapa panjenengan kersa nari?

I'm busy. Kula repot.
No, thank you. Mboten, matur nuwun.
I'd like that. Kula pengin.
That sounds great! Kadosipun saé!
Go away! Panjenengan tinggal!
Stop it! Mandeg rumiyin!

I'm here with my ...
Kula ing ngriki kaliyan … kula.

boyfriend pacar
girlfriend pacar
husband garwa kakung
wife garwa èstri

I'm ...
Kula …

single bujang
married krama
separated pisahan
divorced pegatan
seeing someone taksih pados

Do you like men or women?
Panjenengan remen kakung utawi èstri?

I'm ...
Kula …

bisexual biseksual
heterosexual interseksual
homosexual homoseksual

Can I kiss you?
Punapa pareng kula ngaras panjenengan?

I like you.
Kula remen penjenengan.

I love you.
Kula tresna panjenengan

NATIONALITIES

Where are you from?
Asalipunpanjenengan saking pundi?

I'm from …
Kula saking …

Australia Australia
Canada Kanada
Ireland Irlandia
New Zealand Selandia Baru
the United States Amérika Serikat
the United Kingdom Inggris

I'm …
Kula …

American Piyantun Amérika
Australian Piyantun Australia
Canadian Piyantun Kanada
English Piyantun Inggris
Irish Piyantun Irlandia
a New Zealander Piyantun Selandia Baru
Scottish Piyantun Skotlandia
Welsh Piyantun Wales

Where were you born?
Panjenengan lahir wontenpundi?

I was born in …
Kula lahir wonten …

FAMILY

This is my ...
Punika ... kula.

husband garwa
wife garwa
partner sarimbit

mother ibu
father bapak

older brother mas
younger brother adik
older sister mbak
younger sister adik

grandmother eyang putri
grandfather eyang kakung

aunt bu lik
uncle pak lik
cousin misanan

mother-in-law ibu marasepuh
father-in-law bapak marasepuh
brother-in-law mas ipar
sister-in-law mbak ipar

step-mother ibu tiri
step-father bapak tiri
step-sister mbak tiri
step-brother mas tiri

RELIGION

What religion are you?
Agaminipun panjenengan punapa?

I am …
Kula …

agnostic agnostik
atheist ateis
Buddhist Budha
Catholic Katolik
Christian Kristen
Hindu Hindu
Jewish Yahudi
Muslim Muslim

COMMUNICATIONS

Mail

Where is the post office?
Punapa ing ngriki wonten kantor pos ingkang paling caket?

Is there a mailbox nearby?
Punapa ing ngriki wonten kotak pos ingkang paling celak?

Can I buy stamps?
Punapa kula saged mundhut prangko?

I would like to send a …
Kula pingin ngirim …

letter layang
package/parcel paket
postcard kertu pos

Please send this via …
Nyuwun tulung ngintun punika lumantar …

air mail pos udara
registered mail serat ingkang kadaftar
regular mail serat biasa
priority mail serat kilat

It's going to …
dipun kirim dateng …

the United States Amerika Serikat
Canada Kanada
the United Kingdom Inggris

How much does it cost?
Reginipun pinten?

When will it arrive?
Dumuginipun kapan?

It contains ...
Wosipun ...

What is ...?
Ing pundi ...?

your address
alamat panjenengan?

the address for the hotel
alamat hotel punika?

the address I should have my mail sent to
alamat serat ingkang kedah kula kirim

Can you write down the address for me?
Punapa panjenengan saged nyerataken alamatipun kagem kula?

Is there any mail for me?
Punapa wontenlayang kagem kula?

international internasional
domestic dalam negeri

customs bea cukai

envelope amplop
postage pos
stamp prangko

postal code kode pos

postal insurance asuransi pos

Telecommunications

Where is a pay phone?
Ing pundi wọnten telepon umum?

Can I use your phone?
Punapa kula pareng ngampil telepon panjenengan?

I would like to …
Kula pingin …

> **make an overseas phone call**
> nélpon dateng luar negeri
>
> **make a local call**
> nélpon lokal
>
> **send a fax**
> ngirim faksimili

What number do I dial for …?
Nomer ingkang pundi kagem kula saged ngubungi …?

> **information** informasi
> **an outside line** jalur medal
> **an operator** operator

What is the phone number for the ...?
Pinten nomer telepon kagem ...?

hotel hotel
office kantor
restaurant restoran
embassy kedutaan

What is your ...?
Pinten ... panjenengan?

phone number
nomer telepon

home phone number
nomer telepon griya

work number
nomer telepon kantor

extension (number)
ekstensi

fax number
nomer faksimili

mobile phone number
nomer telepon sèlulèr

Can you write down your number for me?
Punapa saged nyerataken nomer telepon kangge kula?

My number is ...
Nomer kula ...

What is the country code for …?
Punapa kode negara kanggé …?

I would like to buy …
Kula kepingin tumbas …

a domestic phone card
kertu telepon dalam negeri

an international phone card
kertu telepon internasional

a disposable cell phone
telepon sèlulèr sekali pakai

a SIM card
kertu SIM

a mobile phone recharge card
kertu isi ulang telepon sèlulèr

pre-played cell phone
telepon sèlulèr prabayar

What is the cost per minute?
Pinten regi per menit?

I need a phone with XX minutes.
Kula betah telepon xx menit.

How do I make calls?
Kados pundi caranipun nelpon?

collect call
nelpon dipun bayar nomer tujuan

toll-free bèbas pulsa
phone book buku telepon
voicemail pesan suara

On the Phone

Hello?
Halo?

Hello. This is …
Halo. Niki …

May I speak to …?
Saged ngendikan kaliyan …?

> **… isn't here; may I take a message?**
> … mbọten ing ngriki, punapa kula saged ninggalaken pesen?

I would like to leave a message for …
Kula badhe ndèrek pesen kagem …

Sorry, wrong number.
Nyuwun pangapunten, salah sambung.

Please call back later.
Nyuwun tulung ditelepon malih samangké.

I'll call back later.
Kula telepon malih samangké

Bye.
Pareng.

Computers and the Internet

Where is the nearest ...?
Wọnten pundi ... ingkang celak?

Internet café warnet
computer repair shop reparasi komputer

Do you have ...?
Punapa panjenengan kagungan ...?

available computers
computer ingkang saged didamel

(wireless) Internet
internet (nirkabel)

a printer
printer

a scanner
scanner

How do you ...?
Kados pundi panjenengan ...?

turn on this computer
ngurupaken computer niki

log in
mlebet

connect to the wi-fi
kasambung ing wi-fi

type in English
dipun ketik ing basa Inggris

How much does it cost for ...?
Pinten reganipun ...?

15 minutes gangsal welas menit
30 minutes tigang dasa menit
one hour setunggal jam

What is the password?
Punapa kata sandinipun?

My computer ...
Komputer kula ...

doesn't work
mbọten saged didamel

is frozen
macet

won't turn on
mbọten saged murup

crashed
pejah

doesn't have an Internet connection
mbọten kagungan koneksi internet

Windows Windows
Macintosh Macintosh
Linux Linux

computer komputer
laptop leptop

USB port colokan USB
ethernet cable kabel eternet

CD CD
DVD DVD

e-mail e-mail

BUSINESS

Professions and Specializations

What do you do?
Pendamelan panjenengan punapa?

I'm …
Kula …

an accountant akuntan
an administrative assistant pegawé administrasi
an aid worker pekerja sosial
an architect arsitek
an artist seniman
an assistant asisten
a banker pegawé bank
a businessman/businesswoman pengusaha
a carpenter tukang kayu
a CEO direktur
a clerk juru tulis
a consultant konsultan
a construction worker tukang bangunan
a contractor kontraktor
a coordinator koordinator
a dentist dokter gigi
a director direktur
a doctor dokter
an editor èditor
an electrician tukang listrik
an engineer insinyur
an intern magang

a journalist wartawan
a lawyer pengacara
a librarian pustakawan
a manager manajer
a nurse perawat
a politician politisi
a secretary sekretaris
a student siswa
a supervisor pengawas
a teacher guru
a writer penulis

I work in …
Kula nyambut damel ing …

academia akademi
accounting akuntansi
advertising periklanan
the arts seni
banking perbankan
business bisnis
education pawiyatan
engineering insinyur
finance keuangan
government pamarintah
journalism jurnalis
law hukum
manufacturing pegawé pabrik
marketing pemasaran
the medical field bidang mèdis
politics politik
public relations humas

publishing penerbitan
a restaurant restoran
a store toko
social services layanan sosial
the travel industry industri perjalanan

Business Interactions

I have a meeting/appointment with …
Kula wonten rapat/kagungan janji kaliyan …

Where's the …?
Ing pundi …?

business center pusat bisnis
convention hall balé pertemuan
meeting room ruang rapat

Can I have your business card?
Punapa kepareng, kula nyuwun kertu nama panjenengan?

Here's my name card.
Punika kertu nama kula.

I'm here for a …
Kula ing ngriki ajeng …

conference konferensi
meeting rapat
seminar seminar

My name is …
Nami kula …

I work for …
Kula nyambut damel …

May I introduce my colleague …
Punapa pareng kula nepangaken rèncang kerjo kula …

Pleased to meet you.
Remen sanget saged pinanggih panjenengan.

I'm sorry I'm late.
Nyuwun pangapunten kula randhat.

You can reach me at …
Panenengan saged ngubungi kula wonten …

I'm here until …
Kula wonten ngriki dumugi …

I need to …
Kula perlu …

make a photocopy ndamel fotokopi
make a telephone call nelpon
send a fax ngintun faks
send a package (overnight) ngintun paket (sedalu)
use the Internet ngagem internet

It was a pleasure meeting you.
Remen kepanggih panjenengan.

I look forward to meeting with you again.
Kula nenggo pinanggih panjenengan malih.

You Might Hear

Matur nuwun rawuhipun.
Thank you for coming.

Sekedap.
One moment, please.

Punapa panjenengan kagungan janji?
Do you have an appointment?

Kaliyan sinten?
With whom?

Panjenenganipun …
He/She …

taksih rapat
is in a meeting

taksih wonten ing perjalanan bisnis
is on a business trip

taksih liburan
is away on vacation

nembé mawon medal
just stepped out

sawetawis kaliyan panjenengan
will be right with you

badhe kepanggih panjenengan sakpunika
will see you now

Mangga lenggah.
Please have a seat.

Business Vocabulary

advertisement iklan
advertising periklanan
bonus bonus
boss pangarsa
briefcase koper
business bisnis
business card kertu nama
business casual *(dress)* bisnis kasual *(rasukan)*
business plan rancangan bisnis
casual *(dress)* kasual *(rasukan)*
cell phone number nomer telepon selulèr
certification sertifikasi
certified gadhah sertifikat
colleague rencang bisnis
company perusahaan
competition kompetisi
competitor pesaing
computer komputer
conference konferensi
contract kontrak
course kursus
cubicle ruang alit
CV daftar riwayat hidup
deduction deduksi
degree drajad
desk méja
e-mail address alamat e-mail
employee pegawé
employer pangarsa
equal opportunity kalondhangan ingkang sami
expenses béaya

experience pengalaman
fax number nomer faks
field bidang
formal *(dress)* formal *(rasukan)*
full-time wekdal penuh
global global
income penghasilan
income tax pajak penghasilan
insurance asuransi
job pakaryan
joint venture kongsi
license lisènsi
mailing seseratan
marketing pemasaran
meeting rapat
minimum wage upah minimal
multinational multinasional
office kantor
office phone number nomer telpon kantor
paperwork kertas kerja
part-time separo wekdal
printer printer
profession profèsi
professional profèsional
project proyèk
promotion promosi
raise mindak
reimbursement penggantosan béaya
resume daftar riwayat hidup
salary gaji
scanner scanner
seminar seminar
suit setèlan

supervisor pangarsa
tax ID NPWP
tie dasi
trade fair pameran dagang
uniform seragam
union serikat pekerja
visa visa
wages upah
work number nomer kerja
work permit ijin kerja

MEDICAL

At the Doctor's Office

Making a Doctor's Appointment

Can you recommend a good doctor?
Punapa panjenengan saged nyaranaken dokter ingkang sae?

I'd to make an appointment for …
Kula badhe ndamel janji kageem …

today dinten punika
tomorrow mbénjing
next week minggu candhaipun
as soon as possible enggal-enggal

Can the doctor come here?
Punapa saged dokter ingkang ngriki?

What are the office hours?
Tabuh pinten kantoripun buka?

It's urgent.
punika wigati.

I need a doctor who speaks English.
Kula betah dokter ingkang saged basa Inggris.

How long is the wait?
Pinten dangu kedah nengga?

You Might Hear

Punapa eepanjenengan kagungan alergi?
Do you have any allergies?

Punapa eepanjenengan taksih ndamel obat?
Are you on any medications?

Tapak asma wonten ngriki.
Sign here.

Ailments

I have …
Kula gadhah …

allergies alergi
an allergic reaction reaksi alergi
arthritis radang sendi
asthma asma
a backache sakit eegeger
bug bites dipun cokot serangga
chest pain sakit dada
a cold flu
cramps kram
diabetes diabetes
diarrhea diaré
an earache gerah talingan
a fever adem panas
the flu flu

a fracture balung retak
a heart condition sakit jantung
high blood pressure budreg
an infection infeksi
indigestion gangguan pencernaan
low blood pressure darah rendah
pain gerah
a rash bintik-bintik
swelling aboh
a sprain keseléo
a stomachache sakit padharan
sunburn kebrangas
sunstroke kepanasen
a toothache sakit wąją
a urinary tract infection infeksi saluran pipis
a venereal disease penyakit kelamin

I need medication for …
Kula betah obat kanggé …

I'm …
Kula …

anemic kirang rah
bleeding medal rahipun
constipated bebelen
dizzy mumet
having trouble breathing seseg napas
late on my period telat wulan
nauseous mual
pregnant ngandhut
vomiting muntah

You Might Hear

Punikạ ...
It's ...

tugel broken
nular contagious
kénging infeksi infected
keseleyo sprained

I've been sick for ... days.
Kula sampun sakit/mriang ... dinten

It hurts here.
Sakit wonten ngriki.

It's gotten worse/better.
Punika langkung nemen/sae.

Treatments and Instructions

Do I need a prescription medicine?
Punapạ kula betah resep obat?

Can you prescribe a generic drug?
Punapa panjenengan saged maringi obat biasa?

Is this over the counter?
Punapa obat punika disadé bebas?

You Might Hear

Mundhut napas panjang.
Breathe deeply.

Panjenengan watuk.
Cough please.

Nuwun sewu, rasukanipun dipun bikak.
Undress, please.

Punapa wonten mriki sakit?
Does it hurt here?

Tutuk panjenengan dipun bikak.
Open your mouth.

Panjenengan kedah pinanggihan dokter spesialis.
You should see a specialist.

Panjenengan kedah dateng griya sakit.
You must go to the hospital.

Kalih minggu malih dateng ngriki.
Come back in two weeks.

Panjenengan betah tindhak lanjut.
You need a follow-up.

You Might Hear

Panjenengan mbetahaken …
You need …

tes darah a blood test
suntikan an injection
infus an IV
tes strep a strep test
tes urin a urine test

How much do I take?
Pinten ingkang kedah kula unjuk?

How often do I take this?
Kaping pinten kula kedah ngunjuk?

Are there side effects?
Punapa wonten efek sampingipun?

Is this safe for children?
Punapa punika aman kangge lare?

I'm allergic to …
Kula alergi …

anti-inflammatories obat anti radang
aspirin aspirin
codeine kodein
penicillin pinisilin

You Might Hear

Kula nyerat resep … kagem panjeeneengan.
I'm prescribing you …

antibiotik antibiotics
anti infeksi saluran napas anti-virals
salep an ointment
ngicalaken rasa sakit painkillers

Payment and Insurance

I have insurance
Kula gadhah asuransi

Do you accept …?
Punapa panjenengan nampi …?

How much does it cost?
Reginipun pinten?

Can I have an itemized receipt for my insurance please?
Punapa kula saged dipun damelaken nota rinci kagem asuransi kula?

Can I pay by credit card?
Punapa saged kula mbayar ngagem kertu kredit?

Will my insurance cover this?
Punapa asuransi kula nanggung prekawis punika?

At the Optometrist

I need an eye exam.
Kula betah priksa netra.

I've lost …
Kula kicalan …

a lens	lensa
my contacts	lensa kontak
my glasses	kaca paningal

Should I continue to wear these?
Punapa kula kedah terus nganggem punika?

Can I select new frames?
Punapa kula saged milih frame enggal?

How long will it take?
Sepinten dangunipun?

I'm nearsighted/farsighted.
Kula rabun tebih/caket.

At the Dentist

This tooth hurts.
waja punika gerah.

I have a toothache.
Kula gerah waja.

I have a cavity.
Waja kula bolong.

I've lost a filling.
Tambalanipun waja kula copot.

My tooth is broken.
Waja kula tugel.

Can you fix these dentures?
Punapa panjenengan saged ndandosi kerisakan punika?

My teeth are sensitive.
Waja kula sensitif.

You Might Hear

Panjenengan betah tambalan waja.
You need a filling.

Kula badhe nyuntik/mbiyus lokal panjenengan.
I'm giving you an injection/a local anesthetic.

Kula kedah nyabut waja punika.
I have to extract this tooth.

Ampun dhahar punopa-punapa selami … jam.
Don't eat anything for … hours.

At the Gynecologist

I have cramps.
Kula kram.

My period is late.
Haid kula telat.

I have an infection.
Kula kenging infeksi.

I'm on the Pill.
Kula ngunjuk pil.

I'm not pregnant.
Kula mboten ngandhut.

I'm … months pregnant.
Kula ngandhut … wulan.

My last period was …
Haid terakhir kula …

I need …
Kula betah …

a contraceptive kontrasepsi
the morning-after pill pil damel enjing
a pregnancy test tes kehamilan
an STD test tes PMS

At the Pharmacy

Where's the nearest (24-hour) pharmacy?
Wonten pundi apotik 24 jam ingkang paling celak?

What time does the pharmacy open/close?
Jam pinten apotik punika buka/tutup?

Can you fill this prescription?
Punapa panjenengan saged nyerat resèp punika?

How long is the wait?
Pinten dangungipun nengga?

I'll come back for it.
Kula badhé wangsul malih.

What do you recommend for ...?
Punapa saran panejengan kagem ...?

allergies alergi
a cold pilek
a cough watuk
diarrhea diare
a hangover mumet
motion sickness mabuk darat
post-nasal drip tètès grana
a sore throat radang tenggorokan
an upset stomach sakit padharan

Do I need a prescription?
Punapa kula betah resèp?

I'm looking for …
Kula madosi …

Do you have …?
Punapa panjenengan kagungan …?

aftershave krim saksampunipun cukur
anti-diarrheal anti diaré
antiseptic rinse cairan antiseptik
aspirin aspirin
baby wipes tisu bayi
bandages perban
cold medicine obat pilek
a comb jungkat
conditioner kondisioner
condoms kondom
cottonballs bal kapas
dental floss benang kangge ngresiki waja
deodorant deodoran
diapers popok sepindhah telas
gauze perban
a hairbrush sikat rikma
hairspray harspray
hand lotion losion
ibuprofen ibuprofen
insect repellant anti serangga
moisturizer pelembab
mousse mousse
mouthwash penyegar tutuk
razor blades silèt
rubbing alcohol alkohol kangge lècèt
shampoo sampo

You Might See/Hear

Dipun unjuk ...
Take ...

saksampunipun dhahar
after eating

sakderengipun saré
before bed

sakderengipun dhahar
before meals

wektu enjing
in the morning

nalika padharan kosong
on an empty stomach

ditedha
orally

sedinten kaping kalih
twice daily

kaliyan toya ingkang kathah
with plenty of water

shaving cream krim cukur
soap sabun
sunblock krim pelindung matahari
tampons pembalut wanita
a thermometer termometer
throat lozenges pereda radang tenggorokan
tissues tisu
toilet paper tisu kamar siram
a toothbrush sikat waja
toothpaste odol
vitamins vitamin

You Might See

namung dipun kagem teng njawi
for external use only

unjuk sedaya
swallow whole

nyebabaken ngantuk
may cause drowsiness

ampun dicampur alkohol
do not mix with alcohol

PARTS OF THE BODY

abdomen padharan
anus dubur
appendix usus buntu
arm lengen
back pengkeran
belly button puser
bladder kandung kemih
bone tosan
buttocks bokong
breast payudara
chest jaja
ear talingan
elbow sikut
eye netra
face pasuryan
finger racikan
foot ampèyan
gland kelenjar
hair rikma
hand asta
heart jantung
hip bangkèkan
intestines usus halus
jaw kèthèkan
joint sendi
kidney ginjal
knee jengku
knuckles sendi racikan
leg ampèyan
lip lathi
liver ati
lung paru-paru
mouth tutuk
muscle otot
neck jangga
nose grana
penis zakar
rectum dubur
rib unusan
shoulder pamidhangan
skin kulit
stomach padharan
testicles pringsilan
thigh wentis
throat tenggorokan
thumb jempol
toe jempol ampèyan
tooth/teeth waja
tongue lidhah
tonsils amandel
urethra saluran pipis
uterus garba
vagina pawadan
vein pembuluh darah
waist bangkèkan
wrist ugel-ugel

GENERAL EMERGENCIES

Essentials

Help! Tulung!

Fire! Kobongan!

Thief! Maling!

Police! Polisi!

It's an emergency!
Punika dharurat!

Stop!
Mandeg!

Leave me alone!
Tilaraken kula piyambak!

Go away!
Sumingkir!

There's been an accident/attack!
Wonten kecelakaan!

Call ...!
Timbali ...!

> **an ambulance** ambulan
> **a doctor** dokter
> **the fire department** blangwir
> **the police** polisi

Is anyone here ...?
Punapa wonten ... ing ngriki?

> **a doctor** dokter
> **trained in CPR** RJP terlatih

Quickly!
Ènggal-ènggal!

Be careful!
Ngati-ati!

Where is the …?
Wonten pundi …?

American embassy kedutaan Amerika
bathroom pakiwan
hospital griya sakit
police station kantor polisi

Can you help me?
Punapa panjenengan saged mbiyantu kula?

Can I use your phone?
Punapa kula pareng ngampil telepon panjenengan?

I'm lost.
Kula kesasar.

Talking to Police

I've been …
Kula sampun …

assaulted dipun serang
mugged dipun bègal
raped dipun prekosa
robbed dipun rampok
swindled diapusi

That person tried to … me.
Tiyang punika nyobi … kula.

assault nyerang
mug mbegal
rape mrekosa
rob ngrampok

You Might See

Dharurat Emergency	**Griya sakit** Hospital
Polisi Police	**Kantor Polisi** Police Station

I've lost my …
Kula kicalan … kula.

bag(s) tas
credit card kertu kredit
driver's license SIM
identification (ID) KTP
keys kunci
laptop leptop
money arta
passport paspor
purse dompèt
traveler's checks cèk turis
visa visa
wallet dompèt

My … was stolen.
… kula dipun colong.

I need a police report.
Kula betah laporan polisi.

Please show me your badge.
Paringi pirsa lencana panjenengan.

You Might Hear

Kadadosanipun wonten pundi?
Where did this happen?

Jam pinten kadadosanipun?
What time did it occur?

Kados pundi rupanipun?
What does he/she look like?

ngganggu keslarasan
disturbing the peace

pelanggaran lalu lintas
traffic violation

denda parkir
parking fine

tilang amargi ngebut
speeding ticket

nglangkungi wates visa
overstaying your visa

kemalingan
theft

Please take me to your superior/the police station.
Punapa saged kula dipun beta teng atasan panjenengan/kantor polisi.

I have insurance.
Kula gadhah asuransi.

This person won't leave me alone.
Tiyang punika mboten kersa nilar kula piyambakan.

My son/daughter is missing.
Yoga kakung/estri kula ical.

He/She is XX years old.
Piyambakipun yuswa xx tahun.

I last saw the culprit XX minutes/hours ago.
Pungkasan kula mirsani penjahatipun xx menit/jam wau.

What is the problem?
Punapa prekawisipun?

What am I accused of?
Kula dipun tuduh punapa?

I didn't realize that it wasn't allowed.
Kula mboten mangertos bilih punika mboten pareng.

I apologize.
Kula nyuwun pangapunten.

I didn't do anything.
Kula mboten nglampahi napa-napa.

I'm innocent.
Kula mboten lepat.

I need to make a phone call.
Kula betah nelpon.

I want to contact my embassy/consulate.
Kula badhe nelpon dhateng kedutaan/konsulat.

I want to speak to a lawyer.
Kula badhe matur kalihan pengacara.

I speak English.
Kula matur basa Inggris.

I need an interpreter.
Kula betah juru basa.

NUMBERS

Cardinal Numbers

1	setunggal	**17**	pitulas
2	kalih	**18**	wolulas
3	tiga	**19**	sangalas
4	sekawan	**20**	kalih dasa
5	gangsal	**21**	selikur
6	enem	**22**	kalihlikur
7	pitu	**30**	tigang dasa
8	wolu	**31**	tigang dasa setunggal
9	sanga	**32**	tigang dasa kalih
10	sedasa	**40**	sekawan dasa
11	sewelas	**50**	séket
12	kalih welas	**60**	suwidak
13	tiga welas	**70**	pitung dasa
14	sekawanwelas	**80**	wolung dasa
15	gangsalwelas	**90**	sangang dasa
16	enembelas		

100	setunggalatus
101	setunggalatus setunggal
200	kalihatus
500	gangsalatus

1,000	setunggal ewu
10,000	sedasa ewu
100,000	setunggalatus ewu
1,000,000	setunggal yuta

Ordinal Numbers

first	sepindhah
second	kaping kalih
third	kaping tiga
fourth	kaping sekawan
fifth	kaping gangsal
sixth	kaping enem
seventh	kaping pitu
eighth	kaping wolu
ninth	kaping sanga
tenth	kaping sedasa

Fractions

one-quarter	seprapat
one-half	sepalih
three-quarters	tiga per sekawan
one-third	sepertelon
two-thirds	kalih per tiga
all	sedaya
none	mboten wonten

QUANTITY & SIZE

one dozen	setunggal lusin
half a dozen	setengah lusin
a pair of …	sepasang …
a couple of …	sejodho …
some (of) …	pinten-pinten …
a half	setengah
a little	sekedik
a lot	kathah
more	luwih
less	kirang
enough	cekap
not enough	mboten cekap
too many	kekathahen (saged dipun etang)
too much	kekathahen
extra small (XS)	alit sanget
small (S)	alit
medium (M)	menengah
large (L)	wiyar
extra-large (XL)	wiyar sanget
big	ageng
bigger	langkung ageng
biggest	paling ageng
small	alit
smaller	langkung alit
smallest	paling alit

fat	lemu
skinny	kuru
wide	amba
narrow	ciyut
tall	dhuwur
short	cendhèk
long	dawa

WEIGHTS & MEASUREMENTS

inch inci
foot kaki

mile mil
millimeter milimèter
centimeter sentimèter
meter mèter
kilometer kilomèter

milliliter mililiter
liter liter

kilogram kilogram

ounce ons
cup cangkir
pint pint
quart quart
gallon galon

TIMES & DATES

Telling Time

What time is it?
Tabuh pinten sakpunika?

It's 5 A.M./P.M.
Sakpunika tabuh gangsal enjing/sonten.

It's 6 o'clock.
Sakpunika tabuh enem.

It's 6:30.
Sakpunika tabuh setengah pitu.

Five past (three).
Tabuh (tiga) langkung gangsal menit.

Half past (two).
Tabuh (kalih) langkung tigang dasa.

Quarter to (eight).
Tabuh (wolu) kirang seprapat.

Twenty to (four).
Tabuh (sekawan) kirang kalih dasa.

noon rinaa
midnight tengah wengi

early gasik
late telat

In the ...
Ing ...

morning wayah ésuk
afternoon wayah awan
evening wayah sonten

at night wayah wengi
at 1 P.M. ing tabuh setunggal siang
at 3:28 ing tabuh tiga langkungwolulikur menit

A.M. Enjing
P.M. Siang/dalu

Duration

for ...
kanggé ...

one month setunggal wulan
two months kalih wulan
one week setunggal minggu
three weeks tigang minggu
one day sedinten
four days sekawan dinten
one hour setunggal jam
a half hour setengah jam
one minute setunggal menit
five minutes gangsal menit
one second setunggal detik
five seconds gangsal detik

since awit
during sakuntawis

before sak dèrèngipun
after sak sampunipun

one year ago setunggal warsa kepengker
five years ago gangsal warsaa kepengker
six months ago nem wulan kepengker

in two years saklaminipun kalih warsaa
in five months saklaminipun gangsal wulan
in two weeks saklaminipun kalih minggu
in twelve days saklaminipun kalih welas dinten
in three hours saklaminipun tigang jam
in five minutes saklaminipun gangsal menit
in ten seconds saklaminipun sedaasa detik

Relative Dates

yesterday kala wingi
today dinten niki
tomorrow mbénjing
week minggu
month wulan
year warsaa

this week seminggu punikaa
next week minggu ngajeng
last week seminggu kepengker

this month wulan punikaa
next month wulan ngajeng
last month wulan kepengker

this year warsa punikạ
next year warsa ngajeng
last year warsaa kepengker

Days of the Week

Monday Senin
Tuesday Selasa
Wednesday Rebo
Thursday Kemis
Friday Jumuah
Saturday Setu
Sunday Minggu

Months of the Year

January Januari
February Pebruari
March Maret
April April
May Mei
June Juni
July Juli
August Agustus
September September
October Oktober
November Nopember
December Desember

Seasons

Winter Rendheng
Spring Semi
Summer Ketiga
Fall/Autumn Gugur

PLACE NAMES

Countries

Australia Australia
Canada Kanada
England Inggris
Indonesia Indonesia
Ireland Irlandia
Malaysia Malaysia
United Kingdom Inggris Raya
United States of America Amérika Serikat

Cities

United States

Boston Boston
Chicago Chicago
Dallas Dallas
Los Angeles Los Angeles
New York New York

Canada

Toronto Toronto
Vancouver Vancouver

European Union

London London
Paris Paris

Indonesia

Bandung Bandung
Jakarta Jakarta
Purwokerto Purwokerto
Semarang Semarang
Solo Solo
Surakarta Surakarta
Yogyakarta Yogyakarta

www.ingramcontent.com/pod-product-compliance
Lightning Source LLC
Jackson TN
JSHW011400130125
77033JS00023B/766

* 9 7 8 0 7 8 1 8 1 3 2 8 0 *